CASSANDRA A. COLLINS

The
Addicts'
Mom
A Survival Guide

A Financial, Legal and Personal Guide
for Parents of Teens and Adult Children
with Drug and Alcohol Issues

outskirtspress
DENVER, COLORADO

DEDICATION

This book is dedicated to my husband for accompanying me on the wild ride of life and for his constant patience, support and sense of humor. This book is also dedicated to our sons and to our daughter-in-law for the richness they've added to my life, and who make me understand daily the depth with which parents want to protect their children.

ACKNOWLEDGMENTS & SPECIAL THANKS TO:

- The special and talented family and friends who proofread this book and offered valuable and compassionate advice – on writing, on life and on survival, and were always there and consistently supportive and non-judgmental.

- Professionals working within the recovery community whose daily dedication, compassion, strength and commitment with addicts under often thankless, stressful, and emotional conditions returns meaning and opportunity to the lives of addicts and their families.

- Recovering addicts – Those incredible people who feel strongly, love deeply and commit completely – and can apply those attributes to create phenomenal lives for themselves and others when the monkey is off their back.

- Organizations dedicated to returning our criminal justice system to a functional and rational process and who help to rescue those who've become victims of a system gone awry.

CONTENTS

LIST OF INTERNET LINKS –
VISIT WWW.ADDICTSMOMBOOK.COM
(Use of Internet Links allows us to keep information current and to add
to resources available. Documents are available for viewing or printing.)

Treatment Centers, Aftercare Programs & University Programs
Groups and Organizations that Support Recovery
Sample Contracts for Teen or Adult Child Living at Home
Sample Letters to Addicted Child
Durable Financial Power of Attorney
HIPAA (Authorization for Release of Medical Records)
Authorization for Release of Information

THE ADDICTS' MOM

LIFE IS GOOD. For the first time in over 10 years, I have a legitimate feeling that both of our sons are safe. The oldest, Michael, now 26, entered his second treatment for chemical dependency at age 20 and is happily married, in a successful career, happy and safe. Our youngest son, Ben, 24, is completing his second treatment and is doing well in the program.

If anyone had told me that I would be the mother of two sons with drug addictions, I never would have believed them, or even been able to fathom that possibility. If someone had told me that there would actually be some benefits from that experience, for our sons and for my husband and me, I would have defined THAT as insanity.

The experiences over the past decade - before, during and after treatment - stretched us in ways that were unimaginable before this began. There were, and still are, periods of pain, fear, anger and over-whelm. There have also been experiences of great triumph, pride, love, and astonishment. We've learned a lot, and have even more to learn. Insight into my journey may be of help to those beginning that journey now, whether in the initial stages of raising pre-teens or teenagers, or whether your adult child or another loved one is in the full throes of addiction. Each of us has to find our individual path and each situation is different, but if my answers, observations or insights don't help, perhaps the questions I asked will.

When I searched for resources, I found that much of the material written on this subject is written either from the addict's or the professionals' viewpoint. This book is written from the Mom's point of view. I am not professionally trained in this field, and I don't profess to be an expert. I have some life lessons that may sound familiar to some of you and hopefully may help to ease your pain, increase your chances for good outcomes, or let you know that others have experienced some of the same emotions and experiences. I am an attorney by trade, so I have also included information to help in wading through the financial and legal issues that are often part of dealing with addiction.

PART 1 –
THE ADDICTION &
RECOVERY EXPERIENCE
OR
"WHAT THE HELL HAPPENED?"

"Trouble brings experience and experience brings wisdom."
- A favorite fortune cookie

CHAPTER 1

REFLECTIONS

WILL IT EVER stop? Will our lives ever be 'normal'? Were we ever a typical family? Memories of family time keep me sane and warm my heart - group hugs, smiling kids, reading books together, hikes through the woods, wonderful vacations and playing with animals. Animals were always a big part of life - kittens, puppies, horses, llamas and ferrets. Thank God for pictures that remind me of those times, bring back memories, and provide objective proof that we experienced many healthy, fun things as a family. It's easy to forget those times when the craziness of addiction hits.

It all seems like a lifetime ago. Good times didn't just stop, but life evolved until little of our former family existed. Constantly being on guard waiting for the next crisis or battle creeps in gradually and begins to feel normal. That slow decline is devastating, yet difficult to recognize when it's happening. When issues began, my husband and I stuck our heads in the sand and pretended that the issues were just typical kids growing up – young adult issues. I've made that mistake multiple times. Perhaps I'm a slow learner, but when it comes to loving your kids, wanting to help, and wanting to trust – Mom's are masters and I'm no exception.

There was a time when we laughed at the teen escapades. When Ben was 17, he borrowed our pickup truck. We live on a hobby farm where the kids could get a sense of responsibility in caring for animals and could work for their spending money much like I did growing up on a farm. We received a call from the police informing us that our truck had been parked in a residential neighborhood near our house, and they'd been called because of the noise coming from the teenagers in the pickup. As the police approached, the teens ran into the nearby woods, leaving a case of beer in the back of the truck.

We explained that our son had our truck, gave the officers his cell phone number, and asked that they call him and tell him to get back out to the truck. They did, and he complied. Ben was a compliant kid in many ways. He was ticketed for underage drinking. We picked him up, along with the truck. Although we had a discussion with Ben about the incident, my husband and I privately laughed about it. It reminded us of our own teenage adventures on back roads in the Midwest. I remember laughing about Ben being a lousy criminal. We own forty acres within a mile of the neighborhood where they'd parked. Had they gone there and been more discreet, they would never have been discovered that night.

Those were simpler times. I flash to the present. Ben is in treatment battling an Oxycontin addiction. I can't see him today, but my heart and mind are with him. When I think of my little boy, my now very vulnerable 24 year old, I wish I could protect him from the pain of withdrawal and be there to wipe his forehead and hold him, but it's not to be. I know that leaving this to the professionals is in his best interest as well as mine. I've shed some tears, but I'm mostly numb. I forget things, have trouble focusing, and have waves of sorrow, hope, despair, nostalgia and happy memories. Sometimes I can focus on the daily things I need to accomplish where I feel a glimpse of normal. Writing gives me the gift of feeling productive, and helps to put some sanity and logical reflection into the craziness of these days when we know he's in pain, but for the most part, we just need to wait for news from the treatment center.

Addiction typically absorbs the entire family, and writing a book isn't the first thing on the list when parents are living with addiction in the family and desperately trying to find ways to protect and save their children.

For me, it's a little different this time. We're on our fourth round. Two sons – four treatments. The first was a one-week stay for our oldest son, Michael, when he convinced the professionals that his issues didn't warrant the 28-day program. He returned with a more serious addiction the next year. It wasn't the professionals' fault. He was incredibly good at manipulation. Whether the pros were fooled or his addiction had not yet reached levels needing full treatment, when I think about the professionals' conclusion at the time, I second guess myself less about not getting both kids into treatment earlier than we did. Our youngest son, Ben, followed in his brother's footsteps a few years later at age 19, going through a 28-day program followed by an aftercare program in the Midwest. Now, as a 24 year old, he's in treatment again.

It's a reality I could never have envisioned and one I wouldn't wish on anyone. This time I have perspective I didn't have before and although this is Ben's second time in treatment, we know that success – phenomenal success – is possible. Michael went through treatment for Methamphetamine at age 20, and is now happily married, thriving professionally, and is a well-balanced, happy person. The hell we went through earlier has created a special relationship now. He's been a rock and a great resource this time as Ben fights his demons. As Ben progresses through treatment, each time we speak with him, we see more development, peace, and maturity. Ben's emerging as his own person – funny, creative, and caring. We're beginning to see him blossom.

So, now I can write, with the hope that our experiences can ease the pain a bit for other families. I had questions for which I didn't find answers. I wanted to access other parents' stories. Initially, I wasn't always comfortable asking questions or voicing concerns. Developing those skills is one of the unexpected benefits I've received from these experiences.

CHAPTER 2

DETAILS – MIND-NUMBING, EXHAUSTING DETAILS

THERE ARE ALWAYS details–picking up the pieces of a broken life. We try to salvage what's practical so a new start after treatment doesn't begin with so much baggage that progress is impeded. It's important to do this without crossing the line of cleaning up messes so the addict doesn't acknowledge or live with the consequences he created. It's essential that he understand the wreckage and take steps on his own to handle some of the issues when he's well enough to see the reality, and to act to put his life back together. It's a tough line. Deciphering the difference between legitimate help and enabling has been one of my biggest struggles. Initially, I thought enabling included anything I did to help so as I struggled to help, I also constantly carried a robe of guilt. I understand now that the lines are not black and white, and that I can be helpful in some positive ways without enabling. Very gifted professionals and past experience have helped me to distinguish between the two more clearly but this thin line continues to be a constant balancing act.

Steve, my husband and Ben and Michael's father, is driving Ben's car back from Phoenix. We live in the Midwest and helped Ben move to Phoenix two years ago. He's a culinary school graduate with a passion for cooking. He'd dreamed of working at a 4-diamond restaurant there, so we financed his move. Although he did well when he first moved, financing and promoting the move was not one of our better ideas. The addiction likely would have happened anyway. I have no delusions that we could have prevented that, but the distance kept him too far from family and his overall support system. The distance also created tremendous expense for us, with numerous trips to visit which I now have to admit were primarily to check to see that he was functioning. This should have been the first clue that things were *not OK*, but I didn't acknowledge that until we approached the end of the two-year Phoenix debacle. At the time, I just knew that *I* needed to see him on a regular basis for *me* to be able to sleep at night. Now the distance complicates cleaning out the apartment, bringing personal belongings back, and handling the inevitable legal issues created by addiction ranging from criminal drug charges to bill collection issues.

This is the third time Steve and I have sorted and cleaned apartments for our adult sons after they checked into treatment. When they were young, I'd dreamed of the joy of helping them move into new apartments, starting new, exciting times of life. I hadn't envisioned this scenario and I never could have believed it would happen three times.

The first apartment cleaning was after our oldest son, Michael, had been arrested and subsequently admitted to treatment with a Meth addiction. He shared the apartment with his original college dorm roommate who was assigned by the university. We'd later learn that the roommate was a heroin addict. We fought tears as we filled nail holes created by dozens of tiny shelves nailed into the walls. One of the effects of Meth is focusing irrationally on specific things. For Michael, it was nailing little shelves all over the apartment walls.

The second apartment cleaning was after we gave our youngest son, Ben, the choice of treatment or living on the street and losing our support for his completion of culinary school, his lifelong dream. Cleaning that apartment wasn't as traumatic as walking out of it when he still lived there, after giving him the ultimatum when we didn't know which option he'd take. We've learned since that Ben, much like me, makes better decisions after time for thought and after sleeping on it. The nights while he slept on it, I paced and worried that our ultimatum had cost our relationship with our son. As difficult as that was, I knew we couldn't continue to watch him disintegrate. Without help with the addiction, he'd never live his dreams and might not live – period. He eventually made the right choice, promoted by the alternative of home-lessness with no food, money or prospects. He entered his first 28-day treatment. We cleaned the apartment and stored his things.

Now – it's the third apartment cleaning. There wasn't room for me on this trip to Phoenix, as Steve is bringing our son's belongings back in Ben's small car. Steve flew down himself, packed what he could, and is driving back. The solitude for both of us is a good thing, but in a strange way, I miss the closure of cleaning the apartment, scrubbing away the remains of our son's dysfunctional existence in this place.

This time, I needed to stay home, wait for word on how he's do-ing in treatment, and make phone calls and do paperwork to attempt some closure on those aspects of his past life. It's typical stuff when addiction is concerned. First, I note primary concerns to share with the counselor when he calls. In pre-admission calls, based on our prior experiences, I know enough to get to the schedule – visiting hours, dates for family program, processes and timelines – so we can put some semblance of order to our calendar, and hopefully to our lives in some small way.

Despite concerns about detox, for me today's a great improve-ment over the past several weeks. A week passed between the time that we knew the issue was an Oxycontin addiction and the admission date to primary treatment (the 28 day program). *That* was a week of hell. The words on the computer screen from research on Oxycontin haunted me the entire week:

"***How Is Oxycontin Abused?*** *Oxycontin abusers either crush the tablet and ingest or snort it or they dilute it in water and inject it. Crushing or diluting the tablet disarms the timed-release action of the medication, but crushing Oxycontin in this way can give the user a potentially fatal dose.*"

The waiting was horrendous. We knew that he had to make the decision to enter treatment on his own, although our pressure and clear withdrawal of any financial support narrowed his options to being homeless or agreeing to treatment. He told his brother two days earlier than he told us that he was going to go into treatment, and when he finally told us, he still wanted three days to say goodbye to people in Phoenix. It was hard not to panic. Translation of 'good bye' in my mind was one last party that could be dangerous.

It's important to keep some degree of order and control over our own lives, and I've felt some success in achieving that. The exceptions have been the days before admission to treatment and the transition from primary treatment to whatever comes next. When an addict decides to admit himself, my response can't be "Gee, I'm sorry. I had something else planned." So for that week we waited, and waited more, and Steve and I hugged each other, and cried, and fought when the pressure erupted, and supported one another as best we could.

Michael and his wife, Sarah, were aware of what was happening, but until the decision for treatment was made, we didn't inform anyone else. Spreading the worry wouldn't have been productive and could have led to answering questions, using energy that needed to be conserved. So we waited.

Daily, we found an excuse to call so we could hear Ben's voice, to know he was alive and not in jail. On Thursday, he called and said he was ready to be admitted on Sunday. We endured three more nights of anguish worrying about an overdose, an accident, or an arrest prior to his admission for treatment. We considered trying to move up the travel date, but that could have backfired. We decided not to push it, and were unsure of whether that was the best decision – but it was one decision made, and preparations could now be finalized. Much later, we learned that one of those three nights *was* spent in jail.

Addiction complicates even the smallest things. Coordinating logistics for transport to treatment gets complex. If we book a flight that's too early in the day, it increases the chance that he'll miss the flight. If the flight is too late, by the time he gets here it's more likely that withdrawal will begin and we'd prefer check-in at the treatment center before it gets too late. Is he actually capable of getting to the airport and on the plane? We ask how many bags he'll have so we can pre-pay, since we're not sure if he'll have any money. We can't send cash since it could be used to buy more drugs. Credit cards have all been run way over limit and cut off, so we need to pre-pay everything. Should Steve fly there and put him on the plane? Ben doesn't want him to do that so if Steve showed up it could risk an argument and jeopardize entry into treatment. It makes the most sense for Steve & me to meet Ben at the airport and to take him to treatment. Then Steve can fly to Phoenix to drive Ben's car home, filled with the few possessions he's managed to keep. Many things have been pawned, stolen or lost.

The treatment center offers airport pickup, but seeing Ben before he was admitted was important to us. Whether this benefited Ben was not the point. I needed to give him a hug and encouragement before checking him in for detox. At this point, he may not have cared, but I knew that I needed to do this for me, and Ben's history led me to believe that this could be accomplished without high risk. These decisions are highly personal, and what's right in one situation could be a bad option in another situation. In our case, it was essential that Steve was there with me. Ben's a small person so if things got out of hand, Steve could still handle him physically. We didn't anticipate that, but it was within the realm of possibility if he was in withdrawal when he arrived.

As soon as we had a date for admission to treatment, I notified my sister and brother-in-law who live in Arizona. They'd offered to help, but it would be difficult to ask someone else to show up at Ben's apartment, to attempt to get Ben to the airport and on the plane. That also could have backfired with Ben refusing to go if he felt pressured. It was important to me to have them on deck though, in case of emergency.

Ben said one of his roommates had offered to take him to the airport. We attempted to contact the roommate to verify that this was the case but couldn't reach him. Overprotective, maybe, but we had airfare, an admission date, and high risk that treatment wouldn't happen if this flight was missed so we did what we could to increase the chance that he'd be on the plane.

"How responsible is the roommate?" we wondered. We didn't know. Ben had told us that this roommate encouraged him to go into treatment, but at that point, it was very difficult to distinguish the truth from constant lies. Getting himself here, with his roommate taking him to the airport, was to begin his commitment to get clean. We booked the flight and reluctantly decided to depend on Ben's roommate to get him to the airport for a 9:47 a.m. flight.

We didn't push our luck too much. At 7:45, we called to verify that they'd left for the airport. Ben was still in bed. We woke him up. We called the roommate, who didn't answer and never called back. We called Ben again every 5 minutes for the next 20, until it was obvious that he was now awake. We breathed easier when we heard that he was on the way to the airport. He called us when he was at the gate and ready to board. He arrived at the boarding gate 25 minutes before departure. He'd MADE it, so we could breathe at that point. We left for the airport to pick him up, as our drive was similar in length to his flight. Then we began to consider what shape – physically and emotionally – he'd be in when he landed. We reminded each other that the goal today is just to be as supportive as possible, and to get him to the treatment center. If he was rude today, we'd take it. This was not the day for altercation.

Ultimately, Ben arrived, looked tired and was quiet, but it was good to see him and to be able to personally check him into treatment. As we left the treatment center parking lot, we began to breathe again. Our son was safe. We went home to get sleep that hadn't come easily for many days.

Reviewing the minutiae of these plans gives a glimpse into why addicts' families are stressed, exhausted, and confused. Details may vary, but the issues, processes, and financial and emotional costs are consistent. Coordinating admission for treatment is one thing. Living a life like this is craziness – and people trying to help addicts do it *every* day – out of desperation, trying to help and not knowing what else to do. I've done it at various levels. It's crazy, but it's not as simple as those who say 'Don't enable', to draw the lines and stand by while you watch your child disintegrate, potentially hurt other people, or die. The level of craziness and pain involved in dealing with an addict is also the reason that it's essential to establish some lines for yourself, so the addict doesn't completely take over your life long term. The challenge is in determining where to draw those lines.

CHAPTER 3

MARRIAGE

WITH DAILY LIFE centered around damage control and while trying to be empathetic, hopeful and loving toward our son now in treatment, it's easy to be less than thrilled with life. Mental and physical exhaustion and the impact of ongoing stress make it easy to link the misery to my husband. The periodic fantasy of driving away and leaving the stress behind does not always include my spouse in the getaway car. When there's misery (there always is when addiction is involved) and the same person is there throughout the misery, it's easy for me to connect the misery to my spouse. It's difficult to blame the addict, particularly when he's so vulnerable, going through withdrawal and emotional trauma. The needed release is sometimes directed against my husband.

The divorce rate among couples with addicted children ranges from 50-70% -- not surprising with the stress, financial burden and the ongoing emotional trauma. This is tragic, although in some cases may be unavoidable, or depending on personalities, may be the best course. Each situation is unique.

Surviving a child's addiction changes you in both negative and positive ways. My husband, who has endured and survived with me, has an understanding that I will share with no other human being. Hopefully both of our sons will come through the other end of the tunnel and build their lives. When the dust settles, having a spouse with whom celebration, serenity, and 'normal' life can be shared is a great gift that I want to be able to treasure.

When the first treatment for each of our sons wasn't successful, sharing the sorrows and hope that eventually our sons would take steps to recovery was comforting - even when the stress created battles in the marriage. I'm happy that we haven't thrown that away. I came close to doing that, and am thankful daily that I didn't. Steve and I deal with the stress, anxiety, and details very differently and it hasn't been easy and it hasn't been pretty. But for us, it has been worth working through it together.

I found lists and boundaries to be helpful. I've always been the planner in the family, perhaps to an extreme, but when dealing with addiction, planning and prioritization have provided a much needed, albeit somewhat false, sense of control. The lists have helped in dividing duties and keeping the discussions about the many details we encountered objective.

Lists also kept me sane - most days - because days could be lost to crisis or higher priorities depending on calls from treatment counselors, communication with family, calls from creditors, criminal matters, or just not being able to emotionally deal with things that day. The lists and calendars let me quickly differentiate between what could wait until another day and what was essential right now. Transferring things to paper gave me a small sense of control and minimized the degree of stress I felt.

This time around, there's less blame than during Michael's active addiction and treatment. It still raises its ugly head on days when I'm feeling overwhelmed. During these times, I connect the kids' issues with my husband's attention deficit, aversion to pre-planning, and tendency to avoid communication. Living with a spouse with attention deficit can be challenging, particularly when also dealing with kids with addictions.[1] Books and blogs on the topic helped me to understand that challenges in communication, impatience and disorganization were ADD symptoms, rather than a lack of caring on

---

[1]   See Appendix B, What's It Like to Have ADD?

Steve's part. Despite that, during stressful times, it was easy for me to fall into anger and blame.

I was recently reminded that Steve's genetics and personality characteristics were not the sole parental example of rule breaking. I was cleaning out some old files and found my letter to the Dean of Students at the university I attended, explaining my side of why I shouldn't be thrown out of the dorm and put on probation for having a boy (Steve) sitting in my dorm room 45 minutes after visiting hours. Times have changed and I still think my argument against their application of the rules was pretty good, but it reminded me that I haven't exactly colored between the lines myself.

If there's something to genetic propensity, it's not surprising that our sons aren't impressed by authority and don't stay within any box. After recovery, we've seen this used in beneficial ways, but in the throes of addiction, these tendencies are dangerous and can lead to heartbreaking results.

When I'm not in reactive mode, reality trumps blame and I have great appreciation, love and respect for Steve. Unfortunately, these times have been too few in the height of crisis. During the crisis-based lapses, it's easy to forget all that Steve handles. He helps to keep me rational, endured that little road trip from Arizona while I had some down time at home, maintains most things in the house, handles lots of household chores, is my technology guy, and has needed to physically restrain our sons on a few occasions. He's had to put up with my moods and moments of panic and he's done it largely without complaint. In the dark times, even that sets me off. "Why do you hold it in? How can you be so logical? Don't you care? How can you make humor a priority with all that's happening?"

I have been blessed with a loving and logical man but that didn't prevent some major fights and huge issues during stressful times. Under normal circumstances, we balance each other well. His ADD keeps life interesting, his love of adventure keeps life exciting, and his sense of humor keeps me laughing. But at the height of the kids' addictions, his ADD made me feel like I was shouldering the responsibility, his sense of humor just made me angry, and his 'take it in stride' attitude was irritating and made me feel like I should apologize for overreacting. Many of the attributes that balance us well and that attract me to my husband became issues when dealing with addiction.

First time around, I truly didn't know whether we'd survive it. This time, the moments of craziness and blame are fewer, and the moments of appreciation and communication are greater. It's not easy, but we've survived, we've learned, and we've grown.

The benefit of having prior experience as we venture into this fourth entry into treatment is the ability to anticipate and prepare for the emotional toll it takes on us. Steve's been more appreciative of the details I handle, and he's been patient with my volatility. He's taking my moods less personally and has been protective and kind. That's helped me to appreciate all that he does to a much greater degree than before. Those differences, and giving ourselves credit and celebrating the fact that we've weathered these storms despite some bruises allows us to celebrate the victory of surviving – together. We have greater respect, love, and appreciation than ever before. Do we still want to choke each other sometimes? Absolutely. Are we confident that we'll survive this storm, and do we know we're good together? Yes. We've gone through experiences together that either tear you apart or bring you closer. I'm glad that – ultimately – it is the latter.

CHAPTER 4

WHERE DID IT BEGIN?

WHEN OUR SONS were 14 & 16 years old, I dedicated a book I wrote by saying: "This book is dedicated to our sons, who make me understand daily the depth with which parents want to protect their children."

I still feel that way and always will. What I didn't know at that time was the extent of the journey that protection would take and the importance of putting limits on the degree of my protective activities. Watching our babies grow and witnessing the little details that make each of them amazing individuals is a blessing that I'm forever thankful for. When I watch Ben treasure the beauty of food now as a chef, I still see the little boy chopping vegetables, or picking berries and making pies. Trips to the grocery store were always like field trips with Ben, where he educated me about fruits, vegetables and meats I'd never noticed before. I still love grocery shopping with him or going to farmers' markets. He's maintained that fascination and appreciation for the taste, texture and beauty of food that sustains and enhances life.

Ben's connection with animals has also never changed. When he walks in the door, every animal in the house still runs to greet him including the two cats who have typical 'I'll pay attention to you when I feel like it' personalities – except for when Ben comes in the door. He's always had a gentle way with animals. They seem to understand one another.

Ben was selected as a class ambassador in grade school because of his empathetic nature. His responsibility, which he'd taken on naturally before the official appointment, was to make sure that any new student was made to feel welcome and wasn't picked on. Although Ben was a quiet child, he'd speak up for anyone he thought needed help. Others in his class noticed this attribute and reciprocated. Ben was a small child but if anyone picked on him, he had several larger friends who were immediately there to back him up. To my knowledge, he was never in a fight. His personality and his friends never made one necessary. To this day, Ben questions negative statements about other people that are made without facts to back them up. He's called me on a few statements and made me step back and analyze assumptions I'd made. He continues to be quiet but he's an independent thinker and a loyal friend to those close to him.

Ben also has Steve's sense of humor and when he's on a roll can have us cracking up. Even as a youngster, he could point out my absurdity and relieve stress with his humor. When he was about eight years old, we were travelling and I was looking for the map. It turned out that Steve had it in his back pocket. I was less than gracious when I discovered that Steve had what I'd been searching for over the past several minutes. Ben grinned a little, put his hands on his hips and looked at his father and said "Dad, you ignorant scumbag!" For many years, anytime someone in the family was a little more curt than warranted, someone would come out with "Dad, you ignorant scumbag!"

Ben is a loving, empathetic, creative, hard-working, fun person. He often doesn't realize how special he is or give himself credit for his many talents and attributes. He's shown incredible strength in dealing with issues caused by ADD and pain based on several physical issues. In grade school, as an assignment Ben wrote an 'Introducing Myself' Poem. I believe it described him perfectly then and still does.

Ben,
Cool, awesome, nice, and honest,
Brother of Michael,
Lover of animals, archery, and family,
Who feels happy when with pets, friends and family,
and sad when alone,
Who needs company, friends, and family,
Who gives happiness, laughter, and joy,
Who fears getting badly sick, getting badly hurt, and hospitals,
Would like to see peace on earth before I die,
Packers win another Super Bowl,
and to see the world how animals see it.

Our oldest son, Michael's personality is very different from Ben's. They're definitely individuals. We've watched Michael's independent nature grow into a confidence that serves him well. He begged us to convince YMCA camp officials to let him attend camp when he was seven years old, a year earlier than allowed by the rules. He went and came home with exciting stories of catching crayfish and taking a hike through mud up to his waist and loving it. Michael also has a soft touch with animals. In middle school he raised a Warmblood colt – a breed that tends to be very tall. The day after the foal was born we found Michael sitting in the stall with his back against the wall and his feet straight out with the colt lying down with his head fully laid on Michael's lap. The mare (who traditionally would have kept humans at a distance from her baby) was standing next to them, protectively nuzzling the colt *and* Michael. It was the picture of peace and serenity.

When the colt was approaching two years old, I looked out of our bedroom window into the pasture and saw Michael sitting on the back of the untrained colt. No bridle, no saddle – Just Michael on the colt's back. He'd hopped on by climbing onto the top of a tall 4-rail white vinyl fence that divides our yard from the pasture. My heart pounded. This horse had *never* been ridden! I knew if I reacted like I wanted to, running toward him or yelling to let him know he should get off, I could easily spook the horse. Before I could figure out what to do, Michael leaned forward, threw his arms around the horse's neck in a tight hug, swung himself around and dropped to the ground. The horse stood completely still while Michael dismounted. They understood each other.

Later, Michael would spend a summer outside of Yellowstone as a wrangler, taking people from all over the world on trail rides through the Rocky Mountains. He went to great lengths to make sure horse and rider were matched and that the horses were well cared for. The ranch had new owners that year who were inexperienced with horses. There was lots of turnover in wranglers, but Michael was so dedicated to the horses and so determined to succeed that he stuck it out and by the end of the season was the only wrangler left. At that point, he did all of the horse care and ran the rides, despite wearing a cast because of a broken thumb suffered while riding a bronco in the Cody, Wyoming rodeo. He was always hard working, independent, determined, softhearted, empathetic, stubborn, and a risk taker. That can be wonderful, or can be dangerous. We've experienced both results with him.

Although neither of our sons entered formal treatment until after high school, issues began much earlier. By second grade, we realized that Ben was having issues learning to read. At that time, our pediatrician diagnosed him with ADD. Ritalin helped some with reading comprehension, but flattened his personality and negatively impacted his appetite. After about a year, we decided to take him off the Ritalin. His teachers didn't notice any change. Over the years, we tried various medications as well as biofeedback with little success. ADD has been a huge issue for Ben throughout his life.

Since early grade school Ben has also dealt with physical pain. Various professionals told us that the leg pains that were severe enough to wake him up at night were growing pains that would end as his growth slowed. Now, in his mid 20's, the pain still exists. The ADD has also made him accident-prone, so pain issues have increased based on various accidents impacting his knees, hips, back and feet. We've visited physician after physician with no successful resolution. ADD, pain and anxiety put Ben in a high-risk category for chemical dependency.

As our sons approached their teen years, we were focused on helping Ben with ADD and related issues (daily homework was excruciating and difficult for him) as well as building careers and living life. When things began to change with Michael, we should have seen the warning signs. Instead, we saw what we wanted to see and ignored many of the warnings. Additionally, both Steve and I hate altercation. We went to great lengths mentally to avoid what we should have realized were serious issues. As parents, we were world-class rationalizers.

We knew Michael's grades weren't indicative of his ability and also knew he was periodically skipping school. There'd been some drinking and we suspected some minor drug use but we attributed that to typical teenage antics. We didn't approve, but assumed kids just started earlier now and that it was a phase they'd go through. We didn't want to be over-protective, and honestly, reflecting back, we were too busy handling daily issues with the kids and trying to live life and keep businesses going to look at the big picture. We tried our best to handle daily issues, but didn't step back to realize the issues might be serious ones. We were in reactive, not contemplative, mode.

The first undeniable indications that issues were more than normal teen escapades occurred in Michael's junior year of high school. At age 17, early one morning when we thought he was in school, Michael was in a car that rolled. He'd skipped school to party with friends. The car was totaled, and he was lucky to walk away. That same year we were called to the hospital to find Michael in the emergency room with alcohol poisoning. Fortunately, some of the teens at the party where he'd passed out in the bathroom were smart enough to get him to the hospital. Although in a perfect world we would have known where our 17 year old son was, in the real world it's impossible to track a 17 year old at all times. He'd told us he was staying at his friend's house that night. We didn't know he'd be attending a party at a home where the parents were out of town, and that he'd see how many shots he could do based on a dare.

Following the emergency room admission, a drug and alcohol assessment was done and counselors recommended ongoing drug tests. We did this, but later discovered that he'd found ways to beat the tests, so the test results just served to give us a false sense of security. School came easily to Michael so he could get away with skipping school, smoking pot, drinking and not studying and still maintain C's. In hindsight, after the alcohol poisoning some form of treatment would have been beneficial but that was a foreign world to us then. At that time, the world of drug treatment didn't fit into the realm of reality for our family. We thought we were somehow immune from drug addiction. That happened to other families. We were just dealing with a rebellious teen. It would pass. We could handle it. Sometimes the greatest issues in life aren't brought on by the wrong answers, but in the questions we don't face or ask ourselves. We were in denial. We muddled through the rest of Michael's high school years with lots of tension and fear, but he was getting through school and no further full-scale in-your-face emergencies occurred.

The summer after high school graduation we were pleased and relieved when Michael decided to take the job as a wrangler in Wyoming. He wanted the experience, it removed him from the environment of partying friends, and also gave us all some much needed distance from one another. It was hard work, but he loved it. When we visited, we became aware of some beer drinking with the staff at the ranch. It was reasonable social drinking and he was functioning well on the job and overall. He turned 18 that summer, so some social drinking didn't concern us. His life was working.

Despite the high school C's, Michael was accepted into a state college because of his high ACT scores. We were hopeful that attending college would be a fresh start. The summer had been successful and Michael had always been an independent person so it wasn't surprising that he was leaving his high school friends behind and going to a university on his own where he didn't yet know anyone. We thought this was a good sign; A fresh start. Michael moved into the dorms. In his first semester, his GPA was over 3.0 – better than mine had been as a college freshman. He seemed to be adjusting well and enjoying his fresh start. The combination of the summer and first semester confirmed our belief that his high school issues had been teenage challenges that he'd outgrown. He did get an underage drinking citation, but many parents with whom we compared notes said that was not unusual during first year at college.

In the second semester at college, things began to disintegrate. A second underage drinking ticket was followed by a charge for possession of marijuana and drug paraphernalia, and third and fourth underage drinking tickets. By March of that semester, Michael was kicked out of the dorm and his driver's license was revoked. The GPA for that semester ended up at 1.667. At this point, we could no longer ignore the issues. We met with behavioral health specialists who diagnosed Michael as alcohol dependent.

Negotiations with Michael resulted in an agreement to delay treatment. We agreed that if another incident occurred, he would undergo a full chemical dependency assessment comprised of an initial weeklong assessment and admission for a full 28-day program if that was recommended. In June, further issues triggered our agreement and Michael entered a treatment center for a drug and alcohol assessment. After a week, he was discharged with a diagnosis of alcohol and marijuana abuse (not dependence, which is a different level of severity and which would have come with a recommendation to complete a 28 day program). They recommended attendance at two to three AA meetings per week, a sponsor, counseling and abstinence from all drugs and alcohol. If Michael followed through on any of the recommendations, it was minimal and we saw no way to force compliance. He continued to live in his college town, worked in fast food to support himself, and returned to college in fall. The following January, he was suspended from the university due to continued poor academics.

In the meantime, we also began to become more and more concerned about Ben. He'd been struggling with ADD issues since second grade, and scholastics had always been difficult for him. He excelled in hands on, creative areas but the typical school setting required more attention to detail than he was able to give. We tried various medications, none of which seemed to help, and we continued to see him frustrated and depressed by the school challenges. As a high school Junior, Ben was self-medicating to try to control the ADD, and his older brother's influence had exacerbated drug use. We began searching for ways to deal with Ben's scholastic and social issues over and above tutoring and various ADD treatments we'd attempted. We were very worried that he would not graduate from high school.

After researching possibilities, Steve and I decided to visit a boarding school in Arizona that worked with ADD teenagers and offered small group, hands-on classes to complete high school. An added benefit was its location in the middle of a desert where students were secluded and lived within a controlled environment. Class trips kept them associating with the outside world, but the setting provided a degree of control that we felt would benefit Ben. We registered him for the summer program, which would follow his junior year in high school. This would be a good test of the school, and would allow him to make up some high school credits for courses he'd flunked so even if he only spent the summer there, his chances of graduation would be increased.

In mid-summer, our oldest son, Michael, had accepted a job with a construction company. It was incredibly hard physical labor but he was proud of what he was doing. It would be very difficult to maintain this job while using drugs so this seemed to be a good development. When we visited a work site I had concerns about the overall safety of this job for Michael who was slightly over 100 lbs. at the time, but he was dedicated to the job and succeeding. He was in amazing physical shape and was proving to himself and the rest of the crew who were all much larger people than Michael that he could do the job. Sheer determination drove him. There were bets on the crew that he'd quit within his first week. This only drove him more to prove that he could do the job.

After about a month on the construction job, a 1000 pound cage of retaining wall panels fell on Michael, compressing vertebrae in his back and requiring a seven level fusion with two metal rods inserted into his back. In his typical determined way, he was out of the hospital bed in record time and worked hard in rehabilitation for the back, but the realities were frightening, for him and for us. Our 20 year old son with a history of chemical use was now looking at severe pain, months of down time and inability to perform physical work now, and likely to any great extent, in the future. We were no longer naïve. We could see the risk. It was like seeing a train bearing down on us, and not being able to move off the tracks.

We had a trip to California scheduled for Ben to undergo some ADD testing, and then to proceed to Arizona to check him into school for his senior year. The summer session had been successful, so we decided that the Arizona school would be the best option for Ben's senior year.

I'd anticipated that this would be an emotional time. Becoming an empty nester a year prematurely escalated the grief for me of missing the traditional life events and cycles I'd assumed would take place. In my upbringing and in my mind, children lived with their parents throughout high school and celebrated high school graduation in their hometown. It was not to be for us and although I knew this was in Ben's best interest, sending him to Arizona that fall combined feelings of grief, loneliness, anxiety, and guilt. Despite the challenges, I missed him enormously. We had also not anticipated the cost involved with private high school and various trips to and from Arizona for him and for us so that added to the stress.

Michael had recuperated enough following his accident to accompany us on our trip. This was fortunate since we didn't want to leave him at home. We needed to attend Ben's ADD appointment and wanted to take part in checking him in at school, but also wanted to be there for Michael. The only answer was for Michael to come along.

We stayed in a hotel close to a California beach. I remember that night vividly. I didn't sleep well, and by about 4 a.m. I heard Michael crying. He was in pain, and was beginning to internalize the major life changes and long road to recovery facing him because of his accident. I got up and asked if he'd like to take a walk on the beach.

We were in a safe neighborhood, neither of us could just lie there and be quiet, and we also didn't want the whole family awake. Sitting on that beach, sobbing with Michael and watching the sunrise is the greatest contrast I've experienced in my life. The beauty of the ocean sunrise was a strange setting for feeling the intense pain and sorrow that Michael and I felt that night. The consistency of the crashing waves was in stark contrast to the sense at the time that nothing in life was consistent. We talked, we walked, and we cried for hours. After the sun rose, we went back to the hotel room and got a few hours of sleep.

I'd planned a week at a health spa after dropping Ben off. We'd decided that despite Michael's accident, I should stick with my plan. After settling Ben into school, I proceeded to the spa and Steve and Michael flew home. This week was a well-timed blessing, although it's largely a blur. I was too pre-occupied to really benefit from much of the excellent health-related information, but a week of healthy food and some time with my sister who lived in the area was much needed therapy. The spa had a counselor on staff who specialized in life transition, so I met with him. His recommendation was for me to locate a counselor in my home city who could provide ongoing support. I recall trying to surmise what he was actually thinking after my descriptions of my life the past several months, and concluded that 'HOLY SHIT' was part of his internal but unexpressed thought process.

Michael returned to live in his college town. He was now collecting Worker's Compensation payments, he wanted independence and we had no authority to keep him at home. We tried to keep in touch without hovering. By November, we began to get more and more worried. A week went by when we were unable to reach him. I finally drove the hour to his apartment. He answered the door after many rings. He looked terrible, and talked to me in the hallway without letting me in. Despite his appearance, my first thought was that he had a girl in the apartment. Later I'd learn that he'd left his cell phone in his car without noticing and had been in the apartment high on Meth all week, never leaving the apartment.

That same November, Ben was kicked out of the Arizona school. He'd been home for Thanksgiving, had smoked pot with a friend while in our pickup truck, videotaped the experience and then took the video with him when he returned to school. On check-in, the video was discovered and he was kicked out until he could prove to the school that he'd been clean for 30 days. He returned to school in January, and was able to make up missed scholastics so he could still graduate in May.

The first half of the next year continued to be stressful, but Ben was finishing school and Michael's back was feeling better. We didn't realize that the pain was simply being masked by Meth.

Ben's high school graduation was in mid-May. Our plan was to pick Michael up on the way and to do a family road trip to Arizona. That way, we could all celebrate Ben's graduation and then pack Ben's belongings into the van and have a good family trip on the way home. It wasn't to be. Michael called the morning we were to leave and asked that we pick him up at a sub shop that was on the way rather than coming to his apartment. When we arrived, we hardly recognized our son. He was clearly high, his eyes were sunken, and he was pale and was shaking. A police car pulled into the parking lot, and the officers went in to get a sub. Michael descended into massive paranoia.

He'd driven his car to the sub shop and had no intention of coming with us on the trip. He said he'd taken too much pain medication for his back so he was jittery. We later learned that this is what a meth high looks like. We knew he shouldn't be driving his car but also didn't want to leave him alone. He asked us to take him to a friend's house, so Steve drove our van with Michael as a passenger and I followed in his car. Later, we learned that we'd driven him to his Meth dealer's house.

While I drove, I called the treatment center where he'd spent the week last year to see if we could get him admitted. No beds were available. I put his name on a waiting list. It's doubtful whether he would have been willing to be admitted that day anyway, and we hadn't researched any other options for admission. We couldn't delay more or we'd miss Ben's graduation. We considered delaying and flying rather than driving but last minute tickets were expensive and that would leave us no way to move Ben home. We were also unsure whether Michael would allow us to help him in any way at that time. We began the drive to Arizona. What we'd hoped would be a time to connect with our sons turned into a nightmare, feeling stretched between the worlds of our two sons. We tried to compartmentalize and focus on the positive of Ben's graduation, hoping we could come back and get help for Michael.

Throughout that trip, we called Michael daily. Some days he sounded better than others. Then three days before we were to arrive home, he quit answering his phone. We were frantic, imagined the worst and prayed for the best. We also verified that a bed was available at the treatment center. We had no idea what we would be faced with when we got home.

He was alive, but he was in jail and the charges were serious. He'd been arrested for possession with intent to deliver cocaine, psilocybin mushrooms and THC as well as possession of drug paraphernalia. He didn't have Meth in his possession at the time of the arrest. Still, our son could end up in prison for years, and could end up with a felony conviction. Our hearts sank, but he was alive. He still had a future.

We retained a criminal attorney who negotiated delayed prosecution of the charges if Michael entered treatment. Looking at Michael through bars, we gave him the ultimatum. Stay in jail, or if he immediately went to treatment, we'd post bail. Michael's decision was made quickly. He'd go into treatment. It was surreal to go to the bank to get $3000 in cash because the court wouldn't accept a check or credit card. I was used to being the trusted, respected attorney – not an extension of the criminal. I was in a different county so didn't know the staff here, but the demeanor of court personnel and applicable rules were starkly different when dealing with attorneys vs. accused or their families. I took note that in my role as an attorney, I really didn't experience what my clients experienced.

I've always wondered whether Michael's familiarity with the treatment center and the concepts of chemical dependency learned during his week there a year earlier made this step a little less frightening for him. My guess is that it did. Either way, he had little choice. He entered treatment and began his 28 days.

CHAPTER 5

SHARING INFORMATION

WHEN MICHAEL ENTERED treatment, we went through a lot of anguish deciding who should be told and when. We'd never been exposed to drug addiction, treatment or criminal legal issues on this level, so we had no roadmap to follow and we were making decisions during a traumatic period in our lives.

Secrecy creates issues – like hoping people don't notice my red eyes, the 'private' phone calls, the emotional vacancy, and not being able to remember details. Explaining where I was going was an issue both before treatment when we made trips to check on him, and during treatment, for visiting days and the four-day family program offered by the treatment center.

Honestly, there was also reservation based on my own ego. What will people think of me? What kind of mother raises a child with a drug problem? That now seems shallow, but in the initial stages, this *was* a concern. At a time when financial issues were a huge consideration, particularly with the treatment costs, I was also concerned that disclosing information could negatively impact our business. The other issue, and probably the biggest one – is it fair for *us* to decide whom to tell? How much of that should be up to him?

Ultimately, we had to share information with key employees and some family members. We asked Michael if we could share information and he didn't care. Had he answered otherwise, I'm not sure what steps we would have taken. It's likely that we still would've shared information with a few people since we needed emotional support and needed to give rational explanations to those impacted by our physical and emotional absence.

Support and response was mixed although now, as a 'veteran' addicts' mom, I'm feeling less judged. Ultimately, we got better at shielding ourselves from those who weren't supportive, as well as making sure that we weren't reading judgment into people's responses. For many people, as it would have been for me, this is foreign territory. They simply don't know how to respond.

It took a long time before I could appreciate hearing stories other parents would innocently share about their children. It's typical for parents to be proud of their children, but a simple story about a baseball game or a high school concert could make me want to bury my head in a pillow. Emotions varied from being envious and feeling robbed of those experiences that we knew would never be recaptured, to an increase in the ever-present guilt, wondering what those parents had done that we hadn't.

During the years when our lives revolved around treatment, we were very proud of our sons for the strength in all they were doing, but this was difficult to share in general conversation with people who hadn't experienced what we'd been through. It was a different pride than we saw in the parents talking about their kids' sports activity or drama club. This created isolation. We were exhausted, and we simply felt like we were in a different world than our peers.

As time went on and we got more comfortable, we discovered that the more open we were with our experiences, the more frequently we met others who'd been impacted by addiction. It's still the elephant in the room that's often not discussed, but when addiction is brought up it becomes apparent that there are few families today who haven't been impacted by it in some way. When we were ready, we found open discussions to be very therapeutic. Later, when our lives no longer centered primarily on addiction and recovery it became easier to enjoy sharing all aspects of life and to relate to other people again.

CHAPTER 6

PRIMARY TREATMENT & THE TWELVE STEPS

IN THINKING BACK I'm astounded by the level of my naiveté at the time Michael entered treatment. What's now part of our life experience was foreign territory back then. I'd heard there were 12 steps and that treatment was 28 days, so my assumption was about four days for detox, and then two steps a day on average to complete the steps in 28 days. I'd read that one of the steps was the addict's apology to those they'd hurt. What day do we get to that part?

I now understand that years and sometimes decades of the addict's drug use and thought processes aren't turned around in 28 days, and that working the steps is a much longer and in-depth process. That makes the process that much more valuable, but at the time, I wondered about what would actually happen in that 28 days.

My assumption about the four days in detox ended up being pretty close. This varies a great deal depending on the type of drug and the quantity of drug use right before entry. Treatment centers generally do a good job of checking residents out medically. In addition to detox, it's typical for addicts to have ignored their physical health for a very long time. It's important to check this out and to incorporate any necessary steps to deal with other medical issues during the treatment process. If there are pain issues, it's important for the treatment center staff to be aware of that as well.

I can only surmise what the balance of the 28 days includes since I didn't personally experience it. Group and individual counseling are a large part of it, as well as exercise, time to connect with other residents and communicate with other people without drug-induced confidence, eating decent food at regular meal times, and studying. Course work includes the steps as well as learning about the physical and emotional effects of drugs on the body. Various opportunities to share their story are provided, and residents get used to attending AA meetings, both at the Center and outside of it. This gets them comfortable with the meeting process and makes it easier for them to continue attending after in-patient treatment ends. A huge part of treatment is connecting with others who've gone down similar paths, ending the isolation that comes with drug addiction.

Michael attended a center specifically for youth under the age of 25. Ben went to the youth center for his first treatment. Second time around he was on the upper age range, so he opted to go to the adult treatment center.

I'm sure I'm oversimplifying the process and their experience, but what was important to us were the amazing changes we saw on every visit after each of our sons entered the program. Seeing their eyes clear, having two-way communication, and in both cases, seeing obvious weight gain was heartening for us. It was just the beginning, but after months of trying to prepare ourselves for the call about jail, hospital or death, having them in treatment, safe, and making noticeable improvements gave us much needed respite. The newfound hope was a lifeline.

Many resources cover the twelve steps in detail with much more expertise than I can offer so I won't try to duplicate that. For reference, following are the twelve steps of Narcotics Anonymous. These are identical to the twelve steps of Alcoholics Anonymous, except for references to addiction rather than solely to alcohol.

THE TWELVE STEPS OF NARCOTICS ANONYMOUS

1. We admitted we were powerless over our addiction—that our lives had become unmanageable.

2. Came to believe that a Power greater than ourselves could restore us to sanity.

3. Made a decision to turn our will and our lives over to the care of God *as we understood Him.*

4. Made a searching and fearless moral inventory of ourselves.

5. Admitted to God, to ourselves, and to another human being the exact nature of our wrongs.

6. Were entirely ready to have God remove all these defects of character.

7. Humbly asked Him to remove our shortcomings.

8. Made a list of all persons we had harmed, and became willing to make amends to them all.

9. Made direct amends to such people wherever possible, except when to do so would injure them or others.

10. Continued to take personal inventory and when we were wrong promptly admitted it.

11. Sought through prayer and meditation to improve our conscious contact with God, *as we understood Him,* praying only for knowledge of His will for us and the power to carry that out.

12. Having had a spiritual awakening as the result of these Steps, we tried to carry this message to addicts, and to practice these principles in all our affairs.

© A.A. World Services, Inc.

CHAPTER 7

RELIGION & ITS IMPACT ON SELECTING TREATMENT OPTIONS

I'M A SPIRITUAL person, but not a religious one. I respect and somewhat envy those who are active in their places of worship. I believe the community, tradition, and the comfort of faith are priceless. I'm just not able to do it within the context of organized religion. Maybe it began with the constant guilt inherent in my Catholic upbringing, or the vision of the drunken, staggering priest assigned to our small parish, which didn't get the cream of the crop from the ever-shrinking members of the priesthood.

The bloom began to come off of my belief in organized religion and the Catholic Church in particular at the age of five when I spent a week at a Catholic hospital for a kidney infection. The environment was inherently frightening for me at that age with the nun nurses in their foreboding black habits and in my memory, harsh, cold, disciplined manner. My negative perceptions were exacerbated by their duties of giving shots and performing other medical procedures that were frightening to a five year old. This experience likely began my correlation of organized religion with punishment, dictatorial harshness and lack of open communication.

Despite that experience, I attended catechism and church, and did my best to be a good Catholic girl. The ritual of first communion was a positive one, and for a few weeks in third grade (likely inspired by Sally Field's rendition of the smiling, friendly Flying Nun), like most little Catholic girls of that age, I thought maybe being a nun could be a possibility for me. That thought was short-lived.

Sometime in early childhood, the priest taught a segment of our catechism class. I asked a question. I don't remember what it was, but I remember the answer very clearly. In front of my catechism class the priest scolded me and harshly responded "God expects us to have faith, and if you have to ask that, you don't have the faith required by God." For an inquisitive elementary student who believed God gave us minds to use, to develop, and to inquire, this resulted in a retraction from organized religion. Thinking back, this moment triggered two life-changing realizations:

1. That regardless of what this person in an authority position was saying, I had core beliefs that were strong enough to withstand his pressure, and *that* was a gift from God. At that early age, I knew that God had given me a brain, and would not be offended that I was using it to ask questions.

2. That this church was not representing to me what an organization representing God should be.

I later learned that this priest was an active alcoholic. In the final stages before he was finally removed from the church, he would stumble down the middle aisle during services, holding the collection plate, and belittling those who didn't give. At my age, I was unable to separate this representative of the church from the church itself.

Even after this experience, I continued to attend Mass and catechism, but then felt guilty for not 'feeling' God in the church. That changed for me in junior high when a priest who worked at a seminary a few miles away began helping in our parish. He was young, vibrant and positive, and after building trust and courage, I again began asking questions. Rather than belittling or threatening me, he discussed options, he asked what I thought, and he made it clear that asking and thinking was a positive thing and that the answers weren't always clear. I loved those philosophical discussions, and began to have positive experiences and positive feelings about the church. It was then that the final blow took place. My favorite priest was excommunicated for having an affair with a parishioner. I don't know what happened to that priest. I don't condone what he did, but I was very angry with a church based on rules not allowing priests to marry or to live lives that would help them to relate to their parishioners. I began to understand why priesthood didn't always attract emotionally stable men and why there was a shortage of priests, leaving our small parish with less than ideal role models or representatives of the church.

Not long after that, I began skipping catechism; taking rides in the country to fill the time when my parents thought I was attending. This created more guilt. Who skips catechism and then lies about it? – but the pain of the guilt was far less than the pain of the hypocrisy of attending.

Thus began my exodus from organized religion (and an aversion to dysfunctional power structures). Over the years, I tried a few different denominations, but all seemed to want to indoctrinate and use guilt as a tool, so attending always brought more negative to the surface than positive.

When our first son was born, I decided to try church again. This was partly based on wanting him baptized. The indoctrination over the years, despite my skepticism, made me want to have our son baptized, and to carry on the tradition of the baptism and family gathering to celebrate the event. My husband was raised Lutheran so we joined the local Lutheran church. This church allowed its pastors to marry, was less dictatorial, and didn't profess that missing church on a Sunday would condemn you to hell. This was an improvement over the Catholicism of my experience. Michael began Sunday school there when he was five years old. Throughout this period of time, I felt little or no huge negatives, but no closeness to God when attending, and no real connection.

Michael attended Sunday school for several weeks. He was afraid the first week and after the first week, didn't want to go, but we continued to send him. Then, one day at a local Dairy Queen, Michael went from a happy little boy holding ice cream to a terrified, screaming child hiding behind me gripping my legs. I looked up and realized that Michael's Sunday school teacher had just walked in, and that his screams and fear were because he saw her. We never found out what caused the reaction, but we left the Dairy Queen and we left the church. Perhaps it was an excuse, but I didn't want to duplicate my negative experiences in organized religion for my son, and I didn't feel that any of us were benefiting from our church involvement.

Steve's religious background was different than mine. His parents were staunch Lutherans, to the extent of forbidding Steve's brother from going to the prom with a Catholic. Steve's belief system is one of logic, so he's been skeptical of religion since I've known him. He'd joined the church based on my request, so we were in agreement when we decided to leave that church. When visiting grandparents at holidays we attended services at their churches, but other than that, a walk in the woods became our church. There, I felt the presence of a higher power.

Over the years, I've respected and sometimes envied those who've thrived in settings of organized religion. I've seen the benefits of the belief and of the community, and can see the advantages they provide to children raised in that setting. I was never able to let go of the past, and promoting an institution to my children that had caused me pain just didn't feel right. I pray frequently, but don't feel the need to know whether it's to a deity in the sky, or to the clouds, trees, a snowflake or the spirit of animals running in a pasture – all amazing creations by someone or something, which to me is God.

It was with this history that, in desperation and guilt, we began researching drug treatment options for Michael. Reading about the 12 step programs heavily based on the Higher Power initially sent chills down my back. At a time when I needed to trust and needed to make fast decisions, I felt like my choice was a program with much less history and proven success (there are some out there that specifically do not use 12 Steps or Higher Power), or to put my child into what I perceived to be a religion-based program when he was at his most vulnerable. Dissecting information from every source I could find, many sleepless nights and much soul searching led me to Hazelden, a 12 step program, one of the most highly rated treatment facilities in the country, within a few hours of us and with a program specifically for young adults ages 15-25. It was the best fit, and we took the leap of faith. It was one of the best decisions of my life.

For a current list of treatment centers, visit www.addictsmombook. com.

CHAPTER 8

THE FAMILY PROGRAM

MANY TREATMENT CENTERS offer a multi-day program to help family members deal with life impacted by chemical dependency as well as accompanying issues that can arise in addict's families. Family members typically attend this program when the addict is in the 28-day program. We worked on ourselves – not our children. It was refreshing to focus on things that I actually had some control over.

The information was incredibly helpful and spending time with others going through the same trauma, challenges and some victories was therapy we desperately needed. Hearing stories from addicts who were not our sons gave us insight.

Part of the family program was also meeting with our son and his counselor. When each of our sons was in treatment, it was wonderful to be able to be there physically so we could see how much healthier and happier they looked on a daily basis. We attended a total of three family programs – one during each of the full 28-day programs our sons attended. Each was a little different, partly because of variety in programs but also because we were in a different emotional state each time, and the circumstances for each of our sons was also different.

Being able to laugh about the circumstances was refreshing. Addict humor is interesting and gives a much-needed release. An example: The addict's definition of SOBER: Son of a bitch everything's real! It was fun to laugh again. I could physically feel muscles loosening up.

The three C's were discussed. *You didn't cause it, you can't control it, and you can't cure it.* This was a new concept for me when we arrived at the first family program. Initially, I had trouble accepting the concept, especially the 'you didn't cause it' part. After all, when the kids were growing up, if I knew then what I know now, I may have been able to improve our odds.

'You can't control it' was pretty easy to accept. I'd tried that and failed miserably, although those failures hadn't kept me from wearing myself out continuing to try. Hearing that my goal to control it was impossible made it easier to begin letting go of that pursuit. A visual was also helpful. While we were sitting in the classroom, the instructor told us to hold our breath. He had us visualize all the oxygen being sucked out of the room. Next, he said, "Now let me speak to you about giving up breathing and why you shouldn't consider running out of this room to get air." To an addict, expecting him to logically listen to arguments that he should quit taking drugs is like asking us to listen to that instructor asking us not to breathe. That illustration stuck with me, and helped me to understand how irrational it was for me to expect to be able to use reason and logic, trying to convince our son not to use.

'You can't cure it' was an easier one for me. By this time, we'd put our son in the hands of the professionals, and our exhaustion made it easier for us to let go.

By the end of the first family program, I'd come to the conclusion that whether I believed that the three C's are absolutely true was irrelevant to me. Fighting it was unproductive. If I focus on my own guilt or on trying to figure out what I could have done differently, I'm taking focus away from what I can do now. Obsessing about this is counterproductive. Has all that craziness in balancing raising kids and building businesses helped or hurt? Who knows? It has allowed us the financial ability to get great professional help and to help our sons in getting good educations and pursuing dreams. So, to the extent possible, I try not to accept guilt or to focus on what I may have done differently. At the family program, there seems to be a parent for every scenario, and we all feel guilty. I worked too much, I was home too much and coddled him, I was too strict, I wasn't strict enough . . . There was comfort in knowing that, whatever we'd done, we'd be second guessing ourselves.

An unexpected discovery ended any trouble I had in accepting the 'I didn't cause it' belief. While cleaning some files at home after the family program, I located a letter that I'd received from my mother when I was 19, just before I took a three-month van trip through the U.S. The letter had been buried in a file for decades. I have no idea why it happened to turn up at this point. Divine intervention, perhaps.

When I read the letter, I realized how easy it is to forget the thought processes and emotions of our own personal history. I'd remembered that my parents didn't approve of this trip, but had no recollection of their feelings other than that. Reading this letter now, looking at it as a parent, gave me a new perspective on what I'm going through. It also had eerie similarities to the things that had gone through my mind at the family program.

The letter said:

"I'm sorry if I haven't been a good mother. I should have taken more time and not worked all the time but I could give everyone more that way (at least I thought so at the time). Now I realize I was tired and crabby because of too much work and not enough time. It's not easy to be pleasant when everything goes wrong. We've made mistakes all along and are sorry but we have tried so hard to raise our family well. Raising a family isn't easy nowadays."

When I reread this letter after so many years, my heart went out to my mother, but I also realized that with that letter, she'd given me an incredible gift. Reading it, I realized that her perceptions were completely off base, sending a destructive, inaccurate message to me – just as I'd been doing with our sons. First, she was assuming that her parenting was the cause of my desire to travel in a camper van with a young man (now my husband). Secondly, in apologizing for not being a good mother, she was telling me that I was a disappointment to her – that she felt she had somehow ruined me.

This letter helped me to step out of the role of Mom and into the role of our sons. How arrogant it was of me to believe that I had such an impact on them that their drug activities were my responsibility! My sons have a lot of attributes, but blindly listening to anyone, particularly me, was not one of them. How judgmental of me to believe that what I'd done as a parent had somehow damaged them. This was one of my ah-hah moments. Was I playing the martyr role for them, or for me? What possible benefit was there in making the same assumptions about my sons that my mother had made about me? I'm not happy that my children were addicted to drugs and seeing their pain was torture, but who am I to assume that they were so weak that I could have controlled them?

Although my van trip in the 70's was out of the box at the time and caused my parents some sleepless nights, now, over 40 years later, I still remember that trip fondly. I know that it expanded my horizons and that it actually changed my life for the better. Could our sons' experiences, particularly going through treatment, expand their horizons in ways that could be beneficial to them 40 years from now? Do I wish all of us could have escaped going through this? YES! Should I wallow in guilt, and make them feel like I believe I drove them to be failures? Not on your life!

I continue to believe that our actions *do* count – before and now. As parents, we clearly have an impact on our children. Any rational parent alive can look back and find ways that, in hindsight, we could have improved our parenting. Regardless of that fact with all of the areas where I could choose to put my focus when our child is dealing with drug addiction, reliving the past and blaming myself is a poor way to allocate my energy.

Attending the family programs gave me a glimpse into what treatment entails, and helped me to appreciate the emotional, intensely hard work our sons did during their stays there. We were only doing it for a few days, and they did it for months. They ripped apart their lives and changed everything. That takes a lot of strength and courage. We are **very** proud of our sons.

I'm grateful for the insight the family programs gave us. Without those experiences, in some moments it's easy to resent the cost of care, especially when on the surface some of this experience looks like fun -- swimming and outside activities, sitting in a group talking, taking time to think. The degree to which I was emotionally and physically drained after a few days gave me a whole new level of appreciation for the journey our sons have made.

The family program also covered the impact of addiction on the whole family. We looked at six areas of life and compared the addict's experience with our own experience. There were surprising similarities. Here's an example from my notes:

Experience	Him	Me
Physical	Unhealthy, not eating, not sleeping, achy, generally unhealthy	No energy for exercise, lousy diet and weight gain, stress related health issues, sleep issues
Social	Withdrawn, not taking part in activities, restricts friends to users, withdrawn from family, focuses on others' issues rather than his own, focused on drug culture	Feel isolated, resentful and judged, withdrawing from social life and not scheduling events I'd enjoy
Emotional	Unhappy, apathetic, depressed, anxious, dishonest, unwilling to accept personal responsibility, anger, resentment, self-centered/self-absorbed, low self-esteem, blames others	Unhappy, depressed, anxious, mood swings, anger, resentment
Intellectual	Numb, not wanting to think, inability to set goals	No energy for intellectual thought
Academic/Career	Absence from school, low grades, negative attitude, unmotivated to work	Preoccupied with things outside of work, more aversion to professional risk, lack of energy and patience in dealing with employees and clients
Spiritual	Not plugged into feelings	No time or energy for meditation, solo time or spiritual thoughts

This project helped us to realize that addiction impacts the entire family; sometimes in similar ways for the addict and the family. Although some of the phraseology I'd used in describing my emotions and his differed, there were astonishing similarities. On the long road to dealing with addiction, it's typical for the family to begin to take on the characteristics of the addict. Becoming aware of that gave me important insight. This was an important step for me in getting healthy myself.

Another discussion gave me insight into my reactions to our sons' use. I had definitely changed my focus, my standards, and my life. I was letting their drug use direct my own life. It was time to become aware of how and when this was happening and to stop the progression.

Addict	Family
Excuses: I use because . . .	Makes excuses for his use
Tolerance: need more to get same effect	Tolerate intolerable behavior
Drug use creates loss of control	Tries to stop the usage
Obsessed with drugs	Obsessed with addict
Denial: I don't have a problem	Denial: He doesn't have a problem
Isolation: I don't want to see anyone	Isolation: No energy to interact with others
Drug use/withdrawal and feeling terrible becomes normal	Constant stress becomes 'normal'
Blackouts & memory issues	Memory & concentration issues; Emotional burnout

Attending the family programs reinforced the importance of re-gaining control over *my* life, setting boundaries, and accepting what I can't change. I've taken some important steps. This isn't a journey that ends, but I'm feeling like the road's a bit more stable.

Seeing Ben daily while at the last family program, seeing him smile and observing noticeable mental and physical improvement was wonderful. Spending time with other families going through the same anguish and being reminded that this is not our fault significantly lightened the load I'd been carrying. Seeing that addiction strikes people of all backgrounds, religious beliefs, personalities and socio-economic levels helped us to accept that it happens, and made us feel less isolated. The family program group was like a small community who had all lived in the same foreign war-ravaged country so we understood one another with no judgment.

CHAPTER 9

AFTERCARE DECISIONS

THE FAMILY PROGRAM heavily promotes getting control of your own life, but it's difficult to do that when there's little control over scheduling, coordinating, planning finances, or planning our own schedule until the next step in our son's recovery is planned. The sooner we could determine where Ben would go after his 28-day program, the sooner we could focus more on ourselves and living our own lives.

We'd contacted the after-care program Michael had attended so we knew a bed was available, but Ben had not yet agreed to go. Gray Wolf Ranch, an aftercare program in Port Townsend, Washington was our first choice. We trusted them, had seen Michael's success there, and believed it would be a good fit for Ben. While at the family program we met with Ben and the counselor to request a decision by the end of the week. Long ago, we'd registered to attend an out of town multi-day professional conference that would begin in a week, and really wanted to be able to focus while there.

Ben was still trying to manipulate us. First, his response was 'If you make me go to Gray Wolf, I won't go to aftercare at all. I'll go back to Phoenix. Our response was "Good luck walking there." Next was "Hazelden says an aftercare option in the Midwest would be better." Our response: "We'll call you back after we talk to the counselor." The counselor confirmed their recommendation of Gray Wolf. Then came the waiting game. This was the hardest part. Unfortunately, no decision was made before we left the family program but at least our request put considerations on the table earlier than they otherwise would have been.

Michael visited Ben and reported that Ben's objection to Gray Wolf was because they wouldn't allow his cell phone & computer – AHHHH!!! Realistically, this might have been an excuse. Because of his ongoing pain issues, he was petrified that he wouldn't physically be able to do the treks, which are part of the program. He also wanted to be in a city. *We* felt strongly that the slower pace of a smaller town would be beneficial, especially after discharge from the aftercare program. Gray Wolf graduates have the option of staying in the area at a house shared by other grads. This would give Ben the opportunity to work and save money to start his life, while continuing with support from the Gray Wolf resources.

We'd be open to other aftercare programs but not because he would prefer location in California or a program that allows cell phones & computers. We'll pay for aftercare, but not based on mentality similar to vacation planning. If he can show that another location offers what he needs for a successful program, we're open. If not, it's Gray Wolf or no financing from us. It's our money. We have the right to dictate. So – we're back to an ultimatum -- Do what we ask or live on the street. No parent should be put in the position of that ultimatum, and we've had to do it too many times. I lose sleep. I'm an emotional mess. I've relapsed from the plan for my care that I'd designed at the family program. It's important that I step back and focus on my own needs and on what I can control.

So – What do I need? I need to feel like I have some control over my life, relationships, and finances. I need to rebuild confidence that I can dream, plan, and actually experience what's planned. I need to manage my emotions so I have confidence that I can commit to events and social interaction without wanting to cancel because of an emergency or emotional exhaustion.

I understand the concept of relinquishing control and letting Ben make his own decisions. We have no legal or physical control over him, and he has to take responsibility for his own life to recover. However, parents relinquishing control of the addict can be confused with removing the parents' ability to make decisions about things that impact us significantly, such as timing and communication regarding aftercare decisions. I worry about the money, whether there will be conflict, and whether he'll decide to forego aftercare if we don't let him go where he wants. I can't help but have visions of him living on the street. I wonder when and if he'll come home, and how we'll handle that. I try to envision a time when I can feel free to calendar events without concern about cancelling them, or simply not having the energy to participate in life. Until then, how **do** we plan a life?

One way or the other, we'll know within a few weeks. However, being in limbo and anxiety for these few weeks is painful, and I don't feel like I have control over decisions that impact us significantly. I feel powerless and my needs and requests are ignored. I'm resentful of that.

I'd like my stressed out brain to give my memory back, but then I wonder when memories will quit triggering fear.

We head to the conference, not knowing what will happen. Tuesday morning, we finally get the call. Ben acknowledges that he is calling so we can concentrate on our conference. I'm thankful that he's showing consideration and acknowledging our request. He's agreed to go to Gray Wolf, saying that another Hazelden resident, an older chef, said it would be good training. Ben's counselor shares a different version – A group meeting where Ben laid out our ultimatum of Gray Wolf or being homeless. The group asked which he was leaning toward and he responded "Homeless'. They answered, "Dude, have you looked outside?" (This was February in Minnesota.) We take humor where we can find it. Whatever drives him to the right decision is just fine with us.

The next morning, Steve went to an advanced class. I stayed at the hotel, called Hazelden and Gray Wolf to confirm admission and to coordinate timing. I booked a plane ticket for two days after his release from primary treatment. Ben had requested a few days at home before leaving for Washington State. The plane ticket was expensive since we were only a few weeks from discharge date. The next day, the primary treatment center called and recommended a direct transfer from their facility to the airport for a flight to Seattle for a pickup by Gray Wolf. I understood their concerns, but was frustrated that this wasn't discussed prior to my promise to Ben and my booking of plane tickets. It was my fault that I didn't confirm plans with the treatment center before booking, but I was easily irritated those days. I was relieved, though, that the next step was now confirmed. On reflection, I understand that a break between primary treatment and aftercare could be very risky. There's no reason to risk relapse or a change of heart during a visit home, so the flight was moved up for a direct transfer from primary treatment to the aftercare program.

We visited Michael during one evening of the conference and had dinner with a friend of his who's attending law school. He's another successful former resident of Gray Wolf. His parents joined us. Although we don't know them well, there's a bond. When we told them that we're going through the process again, without discussion they know what we're experiencing and their wishes mean a lot. No judgment, no mystery; Just understanding -- a little sorrow for us, but with hope, since we've all been through it with positive outcomes. Sharing an evening with other parents who've gone through this is comforting, and having the next steps in Ben's recovery confirmed leaves us with a sense of peace tonight. We sleep well.

CHAPTER 10

THE AFTERCARE EXPERIENCE

BEN IS SETTLED in at Gray Wolf, an aftercare facility for young men ages 14 to 25 who've completed a primary treatment program or have maintained adequate abstinence from drugs and alcohol. Gray Wolf helps residents to rebuild their lives and learn how to live a sober life-style. The word 'facility' really doesn't describe this place. It's a home and a community.

Primary treatment, simply because it happens immediately after full drug use, must focus on getting the residents through withdrawal, feeling healthy, and beginning to rebuild. Aftercare is all about replacing the old lifestyle with a new one. That goes much further than just taking drugs out of the picture. It's about building a life. If a positive life isn't built, the void left where drug use was will be filled with something. For any of us who've tried to stay on a diet or attempted to change any life pattern, we can understand how difficult it would be for the addict to maintain the new lifestyle if a 28 day program that's completely structured and drug free is followed by a return to the same environment where the drug use flourished. Aftercare fills the residents' lives with honesty, technique, insight and tools for a successful life.

The setting is inspirational. There have been times through our ordeal that I wanted to punish the kids, when seeing them in beautiful places somehow seemed like rewarding them for putting us through hell. The family program made me realize how hard the work of sobriety can be, and helped me to appreciate the benefits of a light and beautiful setting. Gray Wolf isn't fancy, but it's comfortable and set in the green forests outside of Port Townsend, Washington. New residents begin in the main lodge that houses fourteen residents, has a kitchen and a living area including a large room where meetings are held. The reception area, meeting rooms and some of the staff offices are there, too.

As young men progress in their program, they also get to physically move to different bedrooms. In the forest setting there are several buildings, allowing objective goals for physical moves to the next building as the residents achieve personal goals in recovery. Some of the counselor's offices are in yurts in the woods offering privacy and an atmosphere as far from institutional as you can get. Gray Wolf is a family setting where staff and residents get to know each other very well, and longer-term residents are role models for the new arrivals. Each of the residents has lived the manipulative lifestyle of an addict, so they're in a perfect position to call out the new guys when they try to work that manipulation here. It doesn't fly, and there's no peer support for bullshit.

Gray Wolf's Pacific Northwest location is perfect for their trek program, which includes multi-day hiking and kayaking trips. The physical intensity of the treks concerned us since both of our sons had physical limitations -- Michael, because of his serious back injury less than a year before Gray Wolf, and Ben because of ongoing feet, knee, hip and back issues. Ultimately, the treks were a good thing and helped the kids learn how to protect themselves, to ask for help when needed, and to push through and stay strong when appropriate. Hearing stories of Ben's cooking escapades on treks made us laugh. We could envision Ben directing trek participants to gather clams so he could create a feast, or grilling steaks to perfection over the campfire.

The trek experiences were successful in building new appreciation for the little things for both of our sons. An email from Michael shortly after he'd returned from a trek brightened our day.

"It's so nice to be back in society! It's amazing how grateful you can be for the simple things that we take for granted every day when you don't have them for a while. Clean clothes, showers, warm beds, solid food, flushing toilets, groups, ping pong, meetings, company of good friends I hadn't seen for a while, moving vehicles, serenity I get from horses, music, and much, much more."

The program also required the kids to spend some time in the town of Port Townsend, finding things for themselves to do – without cell phones or Ipads. I hadn't considered this before, but for many people and particularly for those in recovery, down time can be dangerous. Today's society doesn't prepare us well to occupy ourselves. For the recovering addict, silence and solitude can create boredom and relapse. Learning to appreciate silence and inactivity is a gift that Gray Wolf gave to our sons and by extension, to us.

Gray Wolf also promoted continuing education, volunteer work, or part time jobs for the residents. This bridged the gap between life as an addict, full time recovery, and return to life in the world. This was a critical part of both of our sons' Gray Wolf experiences. Michael worked at a horse ranch grooming, cleaning stalls, and exercising horses. Seeing pictures of Michael's eyes clear and smiling with his arms around his favorite colt made us smile and brought back fond memories of his horse experiences as a child.

Ben loved helping in the kitchen at Gray Wolf and developed a wonderful relationship with the chef there, who had been through recovery himself. The counselors watched closely to make sure Ben wasn't in the kitchen too much, though. One of his issues is balancing his love of cooking with having a life outside of that, so the setting helped him work on that while letting him enjoy his lifelong passion and rebuild professional confidence.

Gray Wolf has been a lifeline for both of our sons, and also a lifeline for Steve and I. Gray Wolf provided our sons with a place to leave an old lifestyle and develop a new one. I truly believe the personal development they experienced at Gray Wolf has benefited them more than a Harvard education. When we were at a loss as to how to help them, Gray Wolf allowed us to let go and watch them grow. Both of our sons have continued close friendships with many of their Gray Wolf colleagues, and we love seeing the successes of these creative, talented and strong-willed adults who *now* put those talents to *positive* use.

For a current list of aftercare programs, visit www.addictsmombook.com.

CHAPTER 11

LIFE AFTER TREATMENT

THE PATH FOLLOWING Gray Wolf was very different for each of our sons. Ben had already completed culinary school prior to attending Gray Wolf, so he stayed on in Port Townsend to work. Initially he lived at the Wolf Den, a house owned by Gray Wolf that acts as a transition point for young men leaving Gray Wolf who want to stay in the area. Eventually, Ben rented a house outside of Port Townsend.

Ben was hired at an upscale Port Townsend restaurant on Puget Sound. Calls from him during that time made my heart sing. Two months after working there, the owners and the chef left town for a night and put Ben in charge of the kitchen. He called that day, excited and nervous, wanting to share his anticipation with us. He called the next day to report that all had gone well, and to describe his thrill of multi-tasking, having the responsibility, and succeeding. He called the following day, excited to tell us that the owners and chef were pleased, and that they were leaving him in charge again the next weekend. It was great to see him being appreciated for his hard work, talent, and confidence. We were thrilled for him, and thrilled that he was sharing his excitement with us!

We noticed a major change in our sons after their Gray Wolf experiences. They had a new appreciation for life and for things we did for them. We got calls from Ben "Mom, I got your package and I really appreciate it." We'd sent a package of kitchen utensils as a house-warming gift. Appreciation! And he sounds happy!

Several months after Ben's graduation from Gray Wolf, he was thrilled to have an offer to work there as their sous chef. Seeing Ben's name on the Gray Wolf list of staff was a thrill for him and for us. He enjoyed continued contact with this sober community, could be an example to young men just entering the program, and could use his culinary skills in the Gray Wolf kitchen. When he began the sous chef position at Gray Wolf he also helped at the Port Townsend restaurant until they were able to replace him. He loved his full life. "When I leave one job, they don't want me to leave, and when I go to the other job they don't want me to leave – and when I'm not working I know so many people! Last night, after I got off work, I went to a friend's house for dinner. Some friends came over with their kids who played Wii, while we played board games. This is fun!" It warmed our hearts. Ben was not only OK – he was thriving!

This may not seem like a huge development to some parents, but any parent who's watched their child disintegrate in addiction will appreciate the incredible victory these conversations represented. We treasured phone conversations when he was excited about being a renter and having to arrange garbage pickup. He was savoring the independence and the responsibility.

Michael's aftercare situation was different from Ben's. Michael was younger when he completed the Gray Wolf program, and hadn't yet completed college. Returning to a typical college setting is a major issue for young adults completing recovery. The drug and alcohol culture on most college campuses is *not* conducive to recovery. Fortunately, universities exist that have programs that integrate students recently completing treatment into the university setting while providing structure and a peer group that supports recovery.

Augsburg College in Minneapolis, MN was a good choice for us. The Augsburg Step-up program coordinated with Hazelden and Gray Wolf so transition was streamlined and the Step-Up staff already understood what students had experienced in the other programs. Several of Michael's Gray Wolf peers entered the Step-Up program with him,

so he already had a support structure there. Programs are also offered by Texas Tech University, Rutgers, Kennesaw State in Georgia,
Michigan State and Penn State. Visit www.AddictsMomBook.com for
current contact information.

There's a growing trend for universities to offer programs ranging from sober dorms to counseling services to provide support to
students in recovery. Without a program, college campuses are very
difficult environments for recovery.

We were concerned about whether Michael could get admitted
to Augsburg. Although he'd always tested very well, the addiction had
taken its toll on his grade point average both in high school and in his
last two semesters at the state university. We learned that Augsburg
understood that this was typical history for students coming out of treatment, and that they were open minded to applications from students
with varied backgrounds. Michael was required to write an essay presenting why Augsburg should admit him. It was a fun experience seeing Michael excited about returning to college, and focusing on the
essay and his future goals. The essay itself tells his story best, and was
part of getting him admitted to Augsburg and the Step-up Program.
Perhaps this essay will inspire ideas for your son or daughter if an admission essay is required for something they choose to pursue. As we
read the essay, we recognized the son we hadn't seen for several years:

"Learning about Augsburg College and the Step-Up
Program was the answer to a prayer. I completed a 28-day
primary treatment program and am currently in the midst of
my aftercare program. After my completion of Gray Wolf, my
goal is to return to college and complete my undergraduate
degree. The Augsburg Step-Up Program would allow me to do
that in an atmosphere supportive of my recovery.

Continuing my college education is important to me in
several ways. Having injured my back last year limits the vo-
cations I am able to pursue to those dealing with the exercise
of my mind rather than my body. This also ties into many other

goals of mine in continuing my studies in the academic areas I've got such a passion for. In high school, I excelled in math and science. My ACT scores reassured me of that passion and aptitude. I can't wait to challenge myself, especially in those areas, as well as to prove to myself and to Augsburg the extent to which I can excel in my academic career.

My academic history has not always been positive. Although my high school academics had been average, largely due to experimentation with alcohol and marijuana, at the time of my graduation I was determined to become a big success in college. I was also excited about being on my own, and having unlimited freedom. That unlimited freedom began with a college party lifestyle that transformed into a serious chemical dependency. As drug use escalated and caused more and more serious academic issues, I quit caring about academics and decided to work and decide what I wanted to do with my life.

The summer following my sophomore year in college I began working with a construction company building retaining walls. I truly excelled at the construction position. Being the smallest guy in the company, I applied the drive and determination I had to make up for my lack of size. It was the most intense physical labor I'd ever done, which curbed the addiction temporarily. I had a lot of respect from the other workers, and a lot more respect for myself, surprised at what I was able to accomplish.

After about a month of working the construction job, a cage full of retaining wall panels weighing approximately 1000 pounds tipped over, pinning me underneath and leaving me with compressed vertebrae. Luckily, the emergency surgery (a 7-level fusion) was a success, allowing me to walk regularly again. However, needless to say, I wasn't to be returning to work anytime soon. The pain, inability to work, and unlimited free time took me to a new level in my addiction. I swirled into a downward spiral of painkillers and other drugs.

I'm now thankful for the issues caused by the accident, because had I not gotten out of control as much as I did at that time, I may have continued my use and settled to live in mediocrity. That final spiral landed me on Hazelden's doorstep. I learned more in those 28 days than I could have imagined possible. From there, I proceeded to Gray Wolf for my aftercare program, where I continue to learn more about myself every day. I've been sober for nearly four months now, and God willing, I'll have about eight months of sobriety by the time I arrive at Augsburg.

Throughout my treatment process, I've been putting forth the effort needed and excelling, fully knowing that my success with anything else is dependent on maintaining sobriety. I got a true test of how strong my determination and self-motivation can be while working for the construction company, and I'm getting a better sense of how powerful it is here in treatment.

I am confirming within my own mind, as I hope to instill within Augsburg, that I can do anything I set my mind to. I still have the desire to succeed that I have always had, only now I've got a stable mind to turn that desire into reality. I'm excited to continue my education in the way that I was originally meant to, to absorb all the knowledge I can possibly acquire from Augsburg, as well as becoming a great asset to the Augsburg community. The Step-Up Program provides the perfect environment for people in my situation. I hope to help other members of Step-Up with my experience, strength and hope as much as I'm sure they will help me.

My passion for attending Augsburg also extends beyond the benefits of the Step-Up Program. I've become familiar with the twin cities area throughout the last few years, and it's really become a home for me. Being right in the middle of the twin cities, I would be able to experience that area without the necessity of a vehicle. Augsburg's location would enable me to conveniently visit my family in the Midwest. The small class sizes also very much appeal to me, as well as the close-knit community of 1600 students. I look forward to developing close relationships with my peers and professors throughout my stay.

A recovery community intertwined with a college education is a perfect combination to keep my motivation solid and moving in the right direction. I'm looking forward to an incredible experience in continuing my sobriety, restarting my education, and my life."

Michael graduated from the Gray Wolf program in October. We picked him up and enjoyed a road trip from Washington State back to the Midwest. November and December were spent at home, and he began college and the Step-Up program in January. We were nervous before he came home, but with help from counselors we negotiated a written contract with Michael so we all knew what the expectations would be.[2]

Negotiating the agreement highlighted how far we'd come in the relationship with our son. We received an email from him shortly before we picked him up to come home.

"I saw the email that you sent my counselor about the home agreement and I had to laugh. When I talked to you the night before you were saying that you basically wanted to step back and let me get my stuff done, and then the list for the home agreement was two pages long! You're funny! I haven't thoroughly gone over it yet but they all seemed reasonable, except the one censoring my movies and music. We'll have to discuss that one. I'd like to talk about it because the last thing I

---

[2]   See Chapter 23, Negotiating a contract with a teen or adult child living at home, and visit www.AddictsMomBook.com for sample contracts, and for sample letters to an addicted child – one encouraging entering treatment, and another after returning home after treatment, encouraging community service.

want to happen is for us to end up at each others throats about control issues. Not that that's ever happened before. Gotta run. I have dive class, but I'll call you tonight."

We did successfully negotiate the agreement. The ability to anticipate, discuss and agree on issues was a huge step forward. There were still some stressful times during the two months together while we adjusted to the dynamics of our son's return home. Completing treatment and aftercare wasn't a solve-all, and a two-month time period wasn't optimum since it was too long for him to simply be a visitor, yet not enough time for him to get truly involved in the community.

It was a time of adjustment for all of us. Old fears and patterns sometimes crept in. After the intense pain we'd seen our son go through and the pain we'd endured, letting go of fear and control was difficult. Michael was internalizing the changes in his life without the structure of the treatment programs, so it was an adjustment for him, too.

The agreement had required Michael to volunteer. We'd included that mandate in the agreement to give him a feeling of accomplishment, and to continue some structure. When I reflected back to this time now that some years have passed, my memory was initially that those months together were pretty smooth. Reviewing a letter I wrote to Michael reminds me otherwise. For a sample letter to a child not complying with an agreement, and promoting community service, visit www.AddictsMomBook.com. The format of this letter might be useful for any parent in similar circumstances, wanting to communicate to their teenage or adult child. Feel free to use it and other letters provided as a beginning point for your own correspondence.

Despite some challenges, we *did* enjoy spending time together and reestablishing a relationship not overshadowed by drug and alcohol use.

Three years later, Michael graduated from Augsburg College with honors, and by that time, our relationship had greatly improved.

CHAPTER 12

CELEBRATING SUCCESS

THE IMPACT OF our experience with addiction and recovery in terms of our relationships, emotional strength and all we've learned will be life long for our family, and I'm thankful for that. My expectation is that we will continue to see our sons flourish, grow, and enjoy lives not controlled by drugs. The way I now relate to both of our sons is that of a proud mother who trusts each of them to make decisions that will use wisdom gained in the tunnel of addiction, but will encompass all the light and all the expansive options available now that they're out of that tunnel.

Last night was the first time I've been Ben's houseguest. Never before has he lived anywhere that I would've wanted to sleep, and the sleep was restful, sound, and serene. This is a truly beautiful place. I awake in the loft, looking out of big windows framing Puget Sound with a mountain backdrop. It's light, open, and simple. I can't help but contrast this with Ben's last apartment in Arizona where sheets were hung over windows to create perpetual darkness, and where city noises created constant anxiety. I have no doubt that our minds can overcome surroundings, but the surroundings we create also reflect our emotions and mindset. This place, to me, is a testament to Ben's evolution – remaining the witty, twinkly-eyed, creative, compassionate person he's always been, but who's no longer shrouded behind dark sheets and distracting noise.

If this sounds utopian, perhaps it is, and I'll give myself this utopia. I deserve it. I'll allow my bubble, but without expectations that Ben's life and ours will escape the roller coaster of life that all of us experience. The beauty is that I no longer expect the dark drug-crazed tunnel and I'm beginning to let go of the on-guard, tight muscled, constant anticipation of crashes and attempts to detour a train wreck. Instead, this morning, I look forward to three days of 1-on-1 time with my adult son – exploring the Northwest and simply enjoying being together. I treasure this for the gift that it is and I intend to savor every moment by simply being and enjoying – no agenda, no control, and no attempts at anticipating signals of impending doom.

Last night my sister-in-law and my niece who live in the area met me at the restaurant where Ben is working. We enjoyed wonderful food and special desserts sent out by 'Chef Ben' along with his visit to our table to greet and enjoy the guests. Ben's obvious pride in his life, the smile, and the social confidence that was apparent in watching him, along with the obvious respect from his co-workers, make it obvious that they know him well, and enjoy him for who he is. It's a grand night!

CHAPTER 13

CODEPENDENCY

EARLY ON I began to resent the term codependency partly because I couldn't get a grasp on what it was, and partly because it brought up resentment in being told that *I* might have an issue. After the exhaustion of dealing with addiction and ADD, the last thing I wanted to hear was that I needed to work on me. I also perceived references to codependency as suggesting that the effort and help I'd given our sons was a bad thing.

Codependency has various definitions but the one that makes the most sense to me is "the addiction to a supportive role in a relationship." This means living through and for another person, taking care of their needs, trying to fix their problems, feeling constantly anxious about that person and taking on the blame for another person's failures. Codependency is typical in high stress environments like addiction. It can result in the codependent being so focused on others that his or her own needs are ignored.

Ultimately, understanding codependency gave me freedom and made me realize that I actually have control over my own happiness and my own life. Now, I make it a point to re-read material on codependency on a regular basis because it keeps me in check and empowers me in regard to whatever life brings at the time. Early on, coping with our sons' addictions probably would've been easier if I hadn't fought the concepts of codependency so much, but perhaps that was part of the process I needed to go through.

There were so many times that I simply felt that I had no options. What do you do when you see your child disintegrating before your eyes? What options did I have when his demeanor either created hostility or depression in our home? How could I keep those horrible feelings from spreading in our home and into my life? And how DARE the professionals, the books and so many resources infer that I was part of the issue, and that I was controlling or enabling? It seemed that the whole world was sending the message that I was a terrible mother. Even getting professional help resulted in things for me to work on that I didn't feel at the time solved the issue with the kids. On top of all that, I was simply exhausted.

Ultimately, it may have been the exhaustion that made me realize I had to do something differently. Understanding codependency began with the family programs at the treatment center where I started to accept that maybe there was some wisdom that I was missing and perhaps needed. This wasn't a one-time bolt of lightning, but a gradual acceptance and understanding. Now, when I start to feel that I have no options, I know it's time to step back and truly consider the choices that *are* available to me based on what I can personally do. This focuses me on what *I* want and what *I* can do to achieve that, and takes focus off of trying to force others to act in a way that I think is best. I try to consider choices based on the serenity prayer: "God grant me the serenity to accept the things I cannot change; courage to change the things I can; and wisdom to know the difference." The wisdom part still challenges me. It's sometimes hard to know what I do have control over, but when I make decisions based on what I have the power to change and then act on those decisions, it gives me hope, relieves the anxiety and either immediately or eventually helps our sons.

A Tony Robbins workshop had a good illustration. Tony asked an attendee to put up his hand. Tony then put his hand against the attendee's. Tony began to push. The attendee pushed back. He wasn't speaking specifically of codependency, but envisioning this illustration in interactions with our sons helped me to realize that the more I pushed, the more they would push back. When I pushed because I didn't believe they were capable of handling things without my pushing, the pushing was codependence. If my pushing didn't work and their emotions were negative, if I accepted those emotions as my own, that was codependence. When I exhausted myself attempting to anticipate others' feelings so I could 'get ahead' of them and control their feelings, that was codependency. When I felt that in order to be worthy of a relationship I had to be 'needed' and give something to the other person, that was codependency.

Having sons with addictions WAS exhausting, but I ultimately realized that the way I'd learned to deal with it was even more exhausting. Eventually I concluded that the way I'd reacted and tried to protect everyone was not another area where I should beat myself up. I'd developed my codependence honestly, in a loving effort to protect my family and to protect myself. It's natural, when you feel like your world is falling apart, to work very hard to hold it together. Unfortunately, many of the ways that we as human beings try to protect our worlds simply results in putting more pressure on ourselves and less on others, and we do it in ways that can result in unhealthy relationships.

Negative emotions – anxiety, depression, anger, and apathy – are elevated when a person feels that they have no control. It's no wonder that we drive ourselves crazy when we see no way to make things better or feel that whatever we do, things don't improve. I wasn't ready to completely let go of trying to manage (in my mind 'help') everyone else in the family and it's likely that I'll never completely reach that level. When I finally stepped back and decided I had to do something differently, I realized that I *was* ready to prioritize and take steps that I *could* control first. This is simply controlling *me*. Surprisingly, since I reprioritized in this way, I haven't run out of things on the list that I can control, so I seldom get to the point on the list that entails others. It's working much better.

When negative emotions creep in, simply stepping back and

deciding to do what *I can do* without anyone else agreeing or cooperating immediately motivates me and makes me much happier. My conclusion in the moment might be something as simple as taking a walk in the woods or giving someone a hug. It might be reading (or writing) a book, brushing my horses, calling a friend, visiting someone in a nursing home who looks lonely, or petting cats at the local humane association. It might be sitting down with the person who triggered my desire to jump in and 'save' them and simply telling them I love them and asking if there's anything I can do to help – provided that I'm OK if they say 'No Thanks' or if they reject me entirely.

The realization that I can do this has changed my life. Do I master it all the time? No, but knowing that I can control *me* and that I have control over the way I perceive things has truly been a blessing. I live in fear less. I know I can't control the future and I've certainly learned that I can't control other people, but I can control me. This gives me confidence that I can better handle whatever life may throw my way. The family program gave us an alternative Serenity Prayer that's a good reminder for me: *"God grant me the serenity to accept the people I cannot change, the courage to change the one I can, and the wisdom to know it's ME."*

I love to travel. Seeing the world will always be a passion. I love experiencing different cultures and different people and seeing the world. As I began to understand my codependence I understood why travel during the time we were dealing with the kids' addictions was so comforting to me. It was an opportunity to use my insight and interest in other people and other cultures without feeling any responsibility for them. While travelling, it was also much more difficult to feel responsible for everything and everyone at home. I simply needed to apply my travel mentality to my life. Treasure the moments and my surroundings, enjoy people for who they are, celebrate and learn from the differences and pursue the direction that makes me happy. That, in turn, makes those around me happier too.

I believe my greatest difficulty in rejecting my codependent activities was the fear that I was somehow abandoning my family if I quit helping in the way I had been, even when it wasn't working. Letting Go (Author Unknown) from the Hazelden parents' materials, helped me to resolve this.

LETTING GO:

Does not mean to stop caring; it means I cannot do it for someone else

Is not to cut myself off, it is the realization that I cannot control another

Is not to enable, but to allow learning from natural consequences

Is to admit powerlessness, which means the outcome is not in my hands.

Is not to try to change or blame another, it is to make the most of myself.

Is not to care for, but to care about.

Is not to fix, but to be supportive.

Is not to judge, but to allow another to be a human being.

Is not to be in the middle arranging all the outcomes, but to allow others to affect their own destinies.

Is not to be protective, it is to permit another to face reality.

Is not to deny, but to accept.

Is not to nag, scold or argue, but instead to search out my own shortcomings and correct them.

Is not to adjust everything to my desires, but to take each day as it comes and cherish myself in it.

Is not to criticize and regulate, but to try to become what I dream I can be.

Is not to regret the past, but to grow and live for the future.

Is to fear less, and to love more.

With my family, when I consciously began to send the message that I have confidence that they can run their own lives, amazingly they stepped up to the plate and did just that. I'll always have codependent tendencies, but I'm now conscious of it and remind myself frequently to step back, breathe, and to control *me*.

Codependents Anonymous, Inc. (CoDA) has a chart entitled 'Recovery Patterns of Codependence'.[3] The chart is a great synopsis of codependency patterns and recovery. I keep a copy of this in my calendar for a monthly reading. Other excellent resources include the CoDA manual entitled *Co-Dependents Anonymous*, as well as Melody Beattie's book *Codependent No More* and her other books.

---

[3]   See Appendix C, Recovery Patterns of Codependence chart.

CHAPTER 14

ROMANTIC RELATIONSHIPS AFTER TREATMENT

ADDICTS – EVEN recovering ones – scare the hell out of many people. When it comes to parents of daughters who are dating the addict, the fear is elevated. I'd witnessed the Gray Wolf boys who were now in the Step-up program turn into men in their recovery process. As I witnessed their growth, I could truthfully say that if I had a daughter I would have been proud to have her date one of them. Honestly, though, if I hadn't seen the transformation and the heart, strength and wisdom of these guys, if my daughter was dating an addict, their pasts would have scared me, too.

My heart went out to Mark, one of Michael's friends - a thin, quiet man from Texas who'd gone through Gray Wolf a year ago, was in the Step-Up program, and who'd been a guest in our home. It's highly recommended those in recovery refrain from getting into relationships until they've been clean and sober for a year. That eliminates the risk of drama that can be inherent in young relationships and jeopardize recovery, and promotes focus on recovery in the first year.

Mark had waited his year, and had been dating a young woman for a few months when her father approached him and offered him money to stay away from his daughter. Mark didn't take the money, but he was crushed. How humiliating to have someone disapprove so much that they'd try to pay you off? That relationship didn't last for long despite Mark's refusal to accept the money.

The Step-Up program provided a great support system for these challenges. These young men were surrounded by others with similar pasts, similar future goals, and similar obstacles including the ignorance of those whose fear caused them to do hurtful things.

Michael's one-year sobriety anniversary would be May 18th. In mid-May, we visited him in his dorm room and couldn't miss the Cheshire cat smile and twinkling eyes. As soon as we walked in the door he said, "You *have* to listen to this song!" He proceeded to play Rascal Flatt's *'Bless The Broken Road'* (originally by the Nitty Gritty Dirt Band). The lyrics talk about a journey along a broken road that eventually leads to finding the right person.

As soon as the song was over, I looked at Michael and said 'Who is she?' "Sarah", he said. "I met her in religion class." Whoever God is, he definitely has a sense of humor!

Shortly after that conversation, Michael brought Sarah along for a weekend at our cabin. I thought, this is a brave young woman to commit to a full weekend the first time she's meeting the parents. This was our traditional put-in-the-dock-and-open-the-cabin weekend, so Steve and Michael had some hours to work, which gave me lots of time to get to know Sarah. I was delighted.

Sarah was immediately likeable, was obviously close to her family, and was straightforward about things I was wondering, but likely would not have asked that first weekend. "I told him" she said, "that if we're to have a relationship I have to be comfortable that if it doesn't work out, it won't impact your sobriety." Wow! Insightful, straightforward, smart, and independent. We loved her immediately.

Sarah is a down-to-earth woman who fits in wherever she is. She seems comfortable carrying on a conversation with anyone, and is willing to shovel manure or hop on a horse (new experiences for her that she embraced during their initial months of dating). She looks beautiful in an evening gown, can sing and play piano or talk economics and politics. Sarah does not have the rule-breaker personality of our son, nor any history of drug use or addiction. Sarah balances Michael well, softening his intensity in a positive way, challenging him with intellectual conversations and debate, and providing loving support and family that enhances both of them. They'll no doubt have issues like any couple, but they're well matched and we love Sarah deeply.

After meeting Sarah, we wondered how her parents would feel about Michael. He was fortunate that her parents were accepting of him. They were not only gracious, warm, accepting and fun, but are also wonderful role models. Carl and Karen have a consistent strength, an exuberance for life, a love of family, a non-judgmental acceptance of others, and an obvious caring and compassion that's wonderful to be around. We were ecstatic to see Michael accepted by Sarah's family.

Sarah's parents had some experience with chemical dependency. Karen's brother had ongoing issues, had spent some years in jail, and had hurt Karen's parents in many ways. Rather than using this experience to judge or to see Michael's relationship with Sarah in fear, they embraced the work that Michael had done and respected his accomplishments in getting to the place he was currently. Karen's years as a childcare provider gave her insight into enabling, consistency and tough love that were valuable. As we got to know them and they learned more about our family history, they never offered unsolicited advice and we never felt judged, but we greatly respect their opinions and the example they set. Observing Karl and Karen as parents is inspiring. Ultimately, Michael married Sarah, and we feel blessed to have become a part of this extended family.

CHAPTER 15

RECOVERY WISDOM

SINCE MICHAEL'S TREATMENT, he's mentioned several friends who've contacted him – wanting to stop, but without the funds or family support to follow the treatment path that Michael did. One of these was Michael's college roommate, Chad, a heroin addict.

Michael and I did a road trip to pick out a puppy. A year earlier, we'd lost our 13-year-old Sheltie who'd been part of the family since the kids were young. A road trip from Minnesota to Nebraska to pick up Dixie allowed us to get the puppy of our choice, and to spend 1-on-1 Mom and son time together.

Michael lived in the dorms at this point and it was getting late when we arrived back in Minnesota, so we got a pet-friendly hotel to spend the night, and made plans to spend some time together the next day before I headed home. Shortly after arriving at the hotel, Michael's cell phone rang. It was Chad, and he was in crisis. He'd been clean for two weeks and from the end of the conversation that I could hear, was inferring that he needed help and a place to sleep or he was set up for a relapse and God knows what else.

I braced myself for an end of our plans while Michael rescued his friend. What happened next is indelibly burned into my brain as a phenomenal example of wisdom I received from my son.

It was a short phone conversation. Michael was compassionate and completely non-judgmental, but he said "Sorry, I have plans tonight and tomorrow, but the next day we could get together and I'd be happy to help." When he hung up, I quickly offered to get Chad a room, or to make room for him in ours. I said we could adjust our plans, and asked "Shouldn't we help now? He's in crisis. What if something happens to him tonight? What if he relapses again?"

Then came Michael's wisdom in a lightning bolt: "Mom, he's been clean for two weeks. If he can't maintain that without me dropping everything, do you really think he'll stay clean long term anyway? I spent time helping him the last few nights, and I'll check on him tomorrow. I might have handled it differently if he'd been clean for a year or so, but at this point, he needs to be able to take responsibility for himself. Leaning on me every day and expecting me to drop everything else would be unhealthy for both of us."

Boom – in one example, I saw the wisdom Michael had gained through his treatment, which I've since seen him apply in day-to-day life and which I also try to emulate. He respected Chad enough to give him the room to make his own decisions. He was compassionate and willing to help, but not to rescue and wipe out his own plans. He did not take on the problem as his own, and if Chad relapsed or whatever else happened, it was Chad's responsibility – not Michael's. He was not acting in fear.

In that moment, I understood the power of addicts helping addicts and I had a new appreciation for the wisdom my son had gained. He was able to make objective, compassionate choices without giving up his own life, and allow others to make and be responsible for their own choices. I believe that was the beginning of my understanding that Michael was now a leader who had an understanding of life that many never achieve. My relationship with Michael was enhanced that day. I no longer had to hold back and try to decide whether to support something. I was no longer responsible for making decisions for him (as if I ever actually was!) He was now capable of making his own decisions, of saying 'no' when appropriate, and of making decisions based on what he wanted, escaping the pain that can result from living in an attempt to keep everyone else happy. If he could accomplish this, maybe there was hope that I could. This was an important step for me in controlling my codependency.

CHAPTER 16

DID FAMILY HISTORY INCREASE OUR SONS' RISK OF ADDICTION?

I GREW UP in a small town and a big family where it was a moral given that each person and each family produces at least enough to be self-supporting, and where offering others opportunity was the greatest gift you could give. My parents employed many local people on our potato farm. The farm gave me the opportunity to work from a young age. Walking behind the potato digger, picking up dropped potatoes and throwing them to the next row where they'd be picked up by the digger when it came through again was an early job where I could earn money even though I was too young to be allowed on the actual equipment.

When my parents discovered me sick after a night out partying as a teenager, their response was to wake me at 6 a.m. the next day, Saturday morning, to work the potato packager. Pulling potatoes from the conveyor belt into the bag resulted in wet, frozen shirt sleeves. The smell of damp potatoes accompanied by the nausea from the night before required numerous trips to the restroom. The physical anguish accompanied by the embarrassment of the hangover in front of my parents' employees gave me an effective message to think long and hard about doing this again. I yearned for parents like those of my friends, who simply 'yelled' at them. Those friends tended to blame their parents for the discipline. My punishment forced me to accept the results of my own behavior more quickly.

This background helped me to develop a good work ethic and an independent nature. Our kids inherited that ethic. The downside of that foundation is the tendency to overwork and to attempt to handle everything on your own. Asking for help doesn't come naturally to me or to our children. The work ethic, independence and pride in jobs well done have been real assets in our sons recoveries, but also require them to focus on balanced lives, and on asking for help when it's needed. These are areas I need to notice and focus on as well.

As a child, alcohol was a part of life, but was never an issue. Dad, for as long as I can remember, had one single shot of brandy daily. I believe that was part of his longevity. He was in great shape until a few years before his death at 84. Social drinking was accepted and was part of the culture.

My uncle was an issue. He'd been in the front lines in Korea, and had never been the same when he returned. Reflecting back, it's clear to me now that my paternal Grandmother had issues with depression and was a tremendous enabler. Uncle Bob was an alcoholic. I was aware of it and would hear about him being drunk in downtown bars in our little town, but my parents must have made it clear that he was not welcome in our home if he'd been drinking. I'd never seen him drunk until one night when my parents were out of town. My brother Phillip, 12 years older than me, was home from college, staying with us while our parents were gone. He was 19. I was 7.

Uncle Bob came to the door and was clearly drunk. He wanted to come in and my brother told him he needed to leave. He became belligerent and Phillip quickly told me to go to my bedroom. I immediately went and hid under my bed. The bedroom was three rooms away from the front door that entered into the kitchen, where Phillip was speaking with Uncle Bob. The rest is a blur, but I recall hearing arguing and noise that sounded like a struggle. I remained in hiding until Phillip came to get me. When he did, Uncle Bob had left, there was a cut on Phillip's head, and the kitchen floor had blood on it. In my memory, it was a lot of blood, but the memory may not be clear. Perceptions of a 7-year-old girl who'd never experienced anything of this sort may be exaggerated. I'd always idolized my brother, but that day, his pedestal raised a few more feet.

I don't recall discussion of the incident, nor did I ever again see my uncle drunk. In later years, he sobered up and attended family events, but I always felt that his life had little spark. He never married or had a career, and seemed to have little passion for anything. He eventually died alone in a group home in Arizona, where he'd moved to help with some breathing issues he'd developed in later years. That first experience with an alcoholic family member left two lasting impressions. Alcoholism destroys lives, and my grandmother had not been helpful in her relationship with my uncle. She went out of her way to keep him living at home, and didn't believe he could handle working, so discouraged that. At that young age, I didn't know the term enabling, but I knew it when I saw it. That memory was helpful in later years when I needed to be strong. Envisioning either of our sons ending up in any way like Uncle Bob helped to balance that inherent need a Mom has to bailout and enable her children. It didn't work all the time, but I believe that vision of Uncle Bob helped me to curb some of the enabling.

Steve's family background was quite different from mine. Other than holidays, there was little alcohol in his parent's home. His parents had no objection to an occasional cocktail, but the Norwegian culture of his small town was very different than the Irish/Polish culture of mine. Addiction crosses those cultural lines, though. Steve's brother was an alcoholic. Matt had charisma and a degree in Psychology. He was one of my favorite people. Seeing his unleashed talent was exasperating. He was my husband's closest friend throughout his lifetime, and his premature death at age 51 devastated Steve. Matt had moved to the town where we lived and spent a lot of time at our home. Official cause of death was cancer, but the alcoholism clearly had a huge impact on his life and on his death. Steve's mother was also clearly an enabler. I judged her harshly for this until

I struggled with the challenges with our own sons many years later. Remembering the effects of her enabling helped to give me strength when I needed to say no.

The year of Matt's death was also the year that my father died. Dad passed away in March, the same month of Matt's cancer diagnosis. The kids were 15 and 13 and losing these two close family members in one year was difficult for them. This was the worst year of our marriage. I took my father's death hard, and Steve didn't show the empathy I desperately wanted at the time. Steve's focus on Matt contributed to his difficulty in supporting me.

When Matt got sick, Steve asked if Matt could move in with us so we could care for him. I knew this wouldn't be a good situation for the family as a whole. We had two teenagers in the house, I was active in two companies including transitioning one I'd just sold, was getting over Dad's death, and Matt was still drinking. There was no way to know the extent of his needs or the longevity of his battle with cancer. I just knew that I couldn't take it on at that time in my life, and that it wouldn't be a good situation for our kids. I felt that my objections caused some resentment from Steve, and when Matt passed away, I felt shut out. Steve dealt with his grief by pulling inward. It may have been a result of the decision against Matt living with us, or may have just been the way Steve dealt with his grief. Either way, I felt like an outsider at a time in life when I most needed to feel that our family was intact, and I was grieving the loss of both Dad and Matt. This is the year Michael began getting into trouble. Was it environment, genetics, both, or neither?

Many studies show that genetics can increase the risk of addiction. For any of us, if we look at all of the relatives for a few generations, it's highly likely that there'll be some family members with addictions. If we look at decades of our lives, we'll have periods that were less than ideal. So, who knows? It was important to me to think it through. For a while, I tried to find direct causes for our sons' addictions, and I was likely trying to justify blaming Steve. If *his* actions or genetics were to blame, I couldn't have had anything to do with this, right? At this point, it has nothing to do with beating myself or anyone else up. The reality is that the vast majority of our kids' childhoods, as well as mine and Steve's, were pretty ideal.

Steve and I grew up in Midwest small towns in an era when we could take off on our bikes or I on my horse and ride all day. No one had to worry about where we were. Security issues were nearly non-existent. We knew everyone in town. My parents weren't wealthy, but if I wanted a new bike, I had the opportunity to earn it.

The drug culture of the 60's was delayed in coming to our town, so I wasn't exposed to drugs until college. When Steve and I met in the early 70's, pot was prevalent and we smoked regularly. Whether it was due to potency of drugs, a different environment, age of initial use, or variations in body chemistry, the impact of our drug use was far different than the impact of drugs on our sons. Shortly after the undergraduate experience, we evolved out of the drug use phase of our lives.

Although we worked a lot, our kids grew up with two parents who loved them and each other. Because we were self-employed, we were able to be at school functions and to adjust our schedules to spend time with them. We were able to take some wonderful family vacations. Our home is on 40 acres with hiking trails, horses in the barn, and many other animals to play with. Pretty utopian.

So, in trying to find reasons, is it fair to pick out the negative incidents over a few decades to try to find a cause for our sons' addictions? When the kids were born, like any parents, we wanted to protect them and to guide them to lives that would have meaning and joy. We did the best we could. Would I wish addictions on anyone? Absolutely not, but at this point, the experiences of surviving those addictions have created the men that our sons are today, and for that, I'm grateful.

I've wondered sometimes if a more structured and traditional upbringing would have minimized the risk of addiction for our sons. That might be the case, but I'm also proud that we've lived our dreams and shown our sons that they don't have to stay within a box. In a discussion with Michael, I admitted that I seem to be drawn to those people who may accomplish a lot with risk and brilliance, but who could also go the other way and be in a lot of trouble. Michael smiled and said "Mom – you ARE one of those people." Hmm – A compliment or not? He likely recognizes himself in that description as well.

Watching our sons thrive and also watching other recovering addicts as they build their lives makes me realize that the description of 'people who accomplish a lot with risk and brilliance, but who could also go the other way and be in a lot of trouble' clearly defines the addict personality. It doesn't have to be an either/or outcome, though. As I see many of those kids who got in a lot of trouble now turning it around, I swell with pride for them. Unfortunately, some don't make it through the trouble part, and for some, legal or health issues require even harder work to achieve the accomplishment part. For those that do make it through, the experiences are like stretching a rubber band that never returns to its previous size. Their lives are permanently enhanced. Testing limits, and then growing to a point of being able to manage that stretched rubber band creates some amazing human beings.

CHAPTER 17

ADDICTION COMBINED WITH OTHER MEDICAL ISSUES – DUAL DIAGNOSIS

ADDICTION SELDOM EXISTS in a vacuum. It's often combined with attention deficit, depression, anxiety, physical pain and/or other physical or emotional issues. This can create a vicious cycle in diagnosis and treatment. What came first - the underlying issue or the addiction? Was the drug use an attempt to self-medicate the initial condition, or did the addiction and the lifestyle that accompanies drug use create or exacerbate the other condition?

In our case, Ben's ADD and physical pain issues and Michael's back pain from his accident definitely complicated treatment, with the need to balance physical and emotional issues with treatment for chemical dependency. Several attempts at diagnosing and treating Ben's ADD were unsuccessful because symptoms were changed because of drug use. Before admitting Michael to treatment, we wondered if we should just concentrate on trying to get the pain issues resolved first. After a lot of research, it became clear that, until the drug use stopped and the addiction was under control, it would be difficult to make progress on treatment for the pain issues. By the time self-medication transforms into addiction, drug use masks symptoms of other issues, complicating diagnosis and treatment. For that reason, treatment of other issues is typically delayed until the addiction is dealt with first. Treatment facilities do consider dual diagnosis issues, though, so they're aware of all contributing factors and so pain and other challenges don't become unbearable when the drug use ends.

Combining treatment with numerous other tests and medical procedures was sometimes overwhelming, financially and emotionally. Our sons' issues with physical pain also added to concerns about relapse. If physical pain led to addiction in the first place, how could that be controlled without using narcotics? No physician wants to be accused of writing prescriptions for an addict and addicts have to be more careful than the general population about taking addictive medications, so getting appropriate prescriptions and finding other ways of controlling pain can become a challenge. Physical therapy, massage, chiropractic and other types of care can be helpful in some cases, but also may not be covered by insurance, and may not effectively control the pain.

The long medical history that can be a result of addiction can overwhelm families and medical professionals and cloud focus in diagnosis. Symptoms may be mistakenly attributed to the effects of drug use or the negative lifestyle choices that accompany addiction. The same symptoms presented by a non-addict may be taken more seriously or may be easier to spot since symptoms aren't mixed with multiple other issues.

Many in the medical profession are distrustful of addicts. Although there may be legitimate basis for the distrust (physicians are 'conned' by addicts attempting to get prescriptions), this can also create challenges for recovering addicts who have legitimate issues. An addict presenting to a physician, complaining of pain, may simply not be taken seriously with the physician believing that the addict is exaggerating pain simply in an effort to get a prescription.

Physicians risk losing their licenses if authorities believe they've written too many prescriptions, so even if they believe pain medications would be beneficial, they may not be willing to write the prescription. Unfortunately, bureaucrats, rather than physicians, impact patient treatment in this regard. In an attempt to prevent abuse of prescription drugs, restrictions on physicians can actually exacerbate the issue. Not getting appropriate medical treatment can lead to relapse with street drugs as a last effort for pain control if it can't be achieved through legal methods, potentially creating further legal issues and putting the addict back in touch with dealers and other less than desirable contacts.

Multiple issues also add to the complexity of parenting an addict. When other issues exist, we found it difficult to know whether symptoms were created by drug use or by non-addiction related medical issues. It's possible to mistake emotional or physical issues for drug use, believing a relapse has occurred when the symptoms are actually caused by something else. It can also go the other direction. It was sometimes easy for us to make excuses for our sons' actions, blaming it on the other issues, missing evidence of drug use that would otherwise have been more obvious.

When emotional issues impact your son or daughter's communication skills, it can be a challenge for parents to determine when it's appropriate to provide supplementary information. Due to concerns about confidentiality and to protect their own time, some professionals (particularly those that are court mandated) don't offer opportunities for parents to speak with them, even when an adult child is willing to sign a release. When parents are already struggling with the balance between advocating for our children vs. being overinvolved, it can be emotionally draining to decide whether to pursue professionals in order to provide supplementary information. While it's important to respect the professionals' time, particularly with dual diagnosis addicts, it's essential that we be advocates for our children by sharing appropriate information so services provided will be as effective as possible or to prevent criminal sanctions for issues created by medical conditions.

We didn't find any magic answers for dealing with the dual diagnosis, but acknowledging that other conditions accompanied the addiction helped us to understand the importance of coordinating various tests and procedures. Working closely with a family physician who has known our family for a long time has been helpful. Looking at the overall picture helped us to understand our overwhelm and made us realize the importance of supporting one another and staying strong so that, to the extent practical, we could be of help to our sons in all of the areas in which they needed help.

CHAPTER 18

DO WE CHANGE OUR LIFESTYLE? SHOULD WE HAVE ALCOHOL IN THE HOUSE?

BY THE TIME our kids were born we were far past our college era drug use, but we were social drinkers. When Michael entered treatment, we found ourselves questioning how to handle this. Steve and I enjoy an occasional beer, glass of wine, or cocktail, but didn't want to send mixed messages to our son or in any way make recovery more difficult for him.

Instructions for the family program included a rule that no alcohol was to be consumed during those four days, including after hours when we were at the hotel off premises from the treatment center. It's completely logical to have rules to prevent potential issues during a family program when emotions run high. Alcoholism is a genetic disease, so potential for parents to also have addictions increases potential for an issue if parents are drinking. At the time, though, I interpreted this to mean that our drinking at any point was not a good thing. When I had an occasional cocktail I felt guilty, so I simply quit for quite a while. We didn't have a strong desire to use anything even mildly mind-altering at that point, so not having alcohol in the house was not an issue.

Eventually, I came to the conclusion that since alcohol had not created issues for us, our social drinking was fine. Assessing appropriate behavior based on the question "Is it negatively impacting life?" has been a good guideline for our own choices, as well as in deciding whether our sons had an issue at any given time. We did not drink in front of our sons during their early recovery, though. My decision was based somewhat on my experience with dieting. I knew that if I was trying to give up chocolate, it wasn't helpful to have someone eating a candy bar in front of me. I decided to give our sons the same respect and not take any chance that my actions could make maintaining sobriety any more difficult for them. Michael's drug of choice was Meth, but staying away from all drugs and alcohol was essential, partly because drinking or use of any substance could significantly lower his ability to stay away from his drug of choice. It could be a slippery and dangerous slope.

Michael lived at home for the two months between Gray Wolf and Augsburg. Before we left to pick him up, we cleaned all alcohol out of the house. This just seemed prudent. There was no reason to have triggers present.

In discussing whether alcohol should be in the house with our sons, counselors, and others in recovery, I found huge inconsistency in opinions. Michael later said that when people weren't drinking because of him, he felt singled out and embarrassed. It hadn't been helpful in his case. However, counselors shared that they'd witnessed relapses at least partly due to someone in early recovery being tempted around a friend or family member who was drinking. Ultimately, though, it's important for the person in recovery to take responsibility for their own sobriety and to let people know how they can best help. It's important, if someone asks 'permission' to drink that the person in recovery feels comfortable with giving an honest answer, including if that answer is "I'd really prefer that you don't drink in front of me." As time in successful recovery passes, most addicts adjust and get used to being around people who are drinking. In early recovery it may be more risky to be around potential triggers.

Ben's situation was different for us. By the time he graduated from his aftercare program, we'd learned from our experiences with Michael. We'd gotten better about asking our sons what they needed and how we could best support them rather than trying to guess or make judgments for them. The question of whether to have alcohol in our home at that time was also less of an issue because Ben didn't live at home right after completing aftercare. Additionally, he was already around alcohol on a daily basis since he worked in restaurants that included bars.

We worked through the question of alcohol in the house. A bigger question for us was how to handle situations with extended family, particularly when the event would be at someone else's home. My propensity to try too hard to create 'awesome' family experiences during that time was sometimes problematic.

CHAPTER 19

HOLIDAY/EVENT PLANNING

IT'S NATURAL TO want positive, memorable family events and as a Mom, I desperately wanted connection with family, continued traditions, and a sense of normal life for myself and our family. When addiction is present, typical things like planning family gatherings can create major stress. Wanting so badly to have good experiences made me put incredible pressure on myself and others, created knots in my stomach, and caused anxiety around holidays and family gatherings.

I wanted family experiences so badly that I tried way *too* hard - exhaustingly hard - to create positive experiences and events, and then, if they happened, I was too stressed about the outcome to enjoy them. Because I'd pushed so hard, it's likely that others attended out of obligation, tainting the experience.

I was concerned that the addict's behavior would embarrass myself or others so I hovered, sending the message that I didn't trust our sons. When I was preoccupied with monitoring behavior, I was unable to relax and enjoy myself.

Because I was planning, worrying, and hovering while my husband was not, I was sometimes angry and resentful of him and his ability to have fun at family events. I felt like he was oblivious to the issues. It would have been helpful for him to be more aware, but part of the reason that Steve ignored situations was because I created them by trying to force family gatherings and events.

I planned and then cancelled many a family vacation or get-to-gether. I continued to plan family events because I desperately wanted to create the fabric and memories that hold families together, and to have those experiences, but plans were frequently disrupted by addiction-related crisis.

We'd made initial decisions about alcohol in our home, but we struggled with how to handle the presence of alcohol at events in others' homes. For the Christmas following Michael's graduation from aftercare, we requested that alcohol not be present, only to learn later that Michael felt more uncomfortable than if we'd said nothing. The elephant was in the room that Christmas. In hindsight, we should have asked Michael his preference for handling that, shared our concerns with him and come to a mutual agreement that respected all of our wishes. At that time, I hadn't yet evolved to that level. Holiday and family events can be anxiety-ridden for anyone. When addiction is present, anxieties are even stronger. Clear communication is the best practice to minimize the anxiety.

Eventually, life needs to return to real world, protection isn't natural, and those in recovery learn to control their own environments in ways that work best for them personally. Having said that, during or shortly after treatment isn't the time to take the addict into a situation where alcohol is prevalent. In many circumstances, legal issues and constraints prevent the addict from being in those environments anyway.

PART 2 –
LEGAL & FINANCIAL
CONSIDERATIONS OR
"THE PARENTS' SURVIVAL GUIDE"

"Courage is looking fear right in the eye and saying,
"Get the hell out of my way, I've got things to do."
-Unknown

CHAPTER 20

PARENTS' FINANCIAL CONSIDERATIONS

ADDICTION CAN SPELL financial disaster for the addict and for the parents. The cost of treatment is only one of many areas where money can be depleted in dealing with addiction. Many parents have compromised their own retirement or immediate financial security in an effort to save their addicted child. Decisions are often made in a vacuum thinking, "If we help with this, things will be simplified," or "If we cover this, it'll increase his chances for recovery." Those seem to be rational arguments for helping. The problem is that issues crop up daily, and each one increases the financial commitment and the financial risk to you. Helping too much too early or in non-essential ways can deplete resources that may be badly needed later for more productive things, for the addict and for you.

It's also acceptable to acknowledge that you are simply not in a financial position to help. Sobriety comes in many ways, and financial investment brings no guarantees. Decide what you can and are willing to do financially, if anything, set boundaries and prioritize your investment of time and money. Dealing with addiction is incredibly emotional. It's a lousy time to make financial decisions. Using objective guidelines to the extent possible can protect your future. I've suggested some guidelines below but, ultimately, it's a personal decision.

Your personal decisions will be better made, though, if made up front, rather than in reactive mode as things develop daily. Some of this, we learned the hard way. We were fortunate enough to be able to afford excellent treatment facilities and I'm thankful for that. In hindsight, though, we spent a lot of money in totally unproductive, and in some cases destructive, ways in our desperate attempts to protect and save our sons.

If you've been dealing with an addict for a while, my guess is that you've broken some of the 'rules' that we all hear about. There's no contest or awards for doing this perfectly, and dwelling on things we could have done better is counter-productive. The important thing is to proceed with caution and try to keep it as objective as possible because as parents, simply following our gut in these circumstances can compromise our finances and our children's potential for sobriety. The most difficult choice, and ultimately the most loving one, is to cut off financial support when the result is to feed the addiction.

During a family program we attended, an addict visited our group and told her story about going through treatment seven times. I found myself mentally calculating how many treatments we could pay for before we were broke. Later in that session, an extended discussion made me realize that we *could* and *should* set a limit on what we would pay for. Her story also helped us to realize that there are many roads to recovery. She didn't hit bottom and succeed in recovery until she ended up in a dirty, cheap flophouse. Living in a way that even in her drug-induced state was finally unacceptable to her was an essential step in her recovery. There is a difference in treatment centers, and I believe it's worth finding the best. [4] If the best is not attainable, there are other options. I am also absolutely certain that parents should not feel guilty for protecting their own financial security.

We have a power of attorney that Ben had signed earlier, authorizing us to access his financial records and handle financial matters on his behalf. As an attorney with personal experience, I believe that

---

[4]   Visit www.AddictsMomBook.com for a current list of treatment centers and aftercare programs. See Chapter 21 for a discussion of options and methods of financing.

any parent who is financially supplementing an adult child for any purpose should have financial and health care powers of attorney that will allow you to access records and act on your child's behalf. A Release of Information Authorization is also a good idea. If the child isn't willing to sign these, then there should be no financial help. These documents can be a blessing, both for financial monitoring and in emergency situations. In most cases, this will also authorize release of information by educational, medical, and other institutions.[5] Having power of attorney does not obligate you to step in, but allows you to do so if you decide it's necessary.

There are definitely gray areas in making decisions on providing financial help, but in my experience, there are also some lines that should be black and white. We didn't follow them in every instance, but we've regretted it when we didn't.

1. **Areas where <u>no</u> help should be given if there is *any* chance that your child is using:**

    a. Don't pay off bills.

    b. Don't subsidize rent.

    c. Don't help with moving expenses.

    d. Don't give them cash.

    e. Don't fund IRA's.

    f. Don't believe that giving them assets other than cash (e.g., a camera) is any different than cash. It will likely be sold or pawned to cover drug-related expenses, or may mysteriously disappear from apartments frequented by transient, unsavory individuals.

    g. Don't cover legal fees UNLESS your child enters treatment as a pre-requisite. Don't pay fees until they have actually entered treatment. If they're in jail, don't pay bail unless they'll be going directly from jail to treatment.

---

[5] See Chapter 22, Legal Considerations – Estate Planning for more discussion. Power of Attorney, HIPAA form and Authorization for Release of Information may be viewed and printed at www.AddictsMomBook.com.

h. Don't pay off principal of outstanding debt, even if your child is in recovery. Coming out of treatment with fresh credit lines open is not helpful.

I wish I'd had this list posted on the refrigerator or attached to our checkbook and credit card when we were going through the ordeals with each of our sons. I finally found the strength to say no to writing checks for the type of expenses listed above when I began to visualize any funds we supplied in these areas as going directly to the dealer to feed the addiction. If you pay for one thing, it frees cash for drugs, so ultimately you're feeding the habit.

I found the desire to personally pay the bills to be overwhelming at times, convincing myself that he would be fine if he wasn't under such financial pressure. After all, working too many hours adds stress. Could that be escalating the need to use the drugs? And, if he was broke, he might deal and really end up with legal issues. I now know that these were flawed thought processes. Until the addiction is under control, money issues will never be solved regardless of how much help is given, and fewer money issues can delay hitting bottom. The longer it takes to hit bottom, the more severe and dangerous the addiction. An addict's drug use will escalate, and if they're going to deal, it will happen. My initial rationalizations were destructive, to our sons and to us.

I also felt personal guilt seeing creditors take losses, but eventually learned that it wasn't productive for me to stress over this. This is likely why I felt the need and found some solace in making sure the apartments were cleaned. Cleaning the apartments and eliminating some of those expenses worked for us. We could afford the time, protected the landlord to some degree, and the scrubbing was therapeutic. Picking and choosing what works for you is important, but give yourself credit for what you do, and don't beat yourself up for not being able to wave a magic wand and make it all better. As parents with addicted children, we don't celebrate our small successes nearly enough.

2. **Areas where it makes sense to take steps *if you choose to after* a child enters treatment (or jail), to minimize charges that will pile up for no purpose:**

These are personal decisions and should only be done if you have the time, money and/or energy for it. A power of attorney or other legal authorization will also be required from your adult child before you may take many of these steps.[6] Having an objective list may be helpful in prioritizing damage control while not stepping over the line into enabling.

   a. Take possession of any vehicles, park them and cancel insurance, provided you're sure no one will be driving the vehicle. Taking possession of vehicles eliminates the risk of someone else driving the car and having an accident, while saving unnecessary insurance premiums. Be certain that insurance is reinstated before the vehicle is driven again.

   b. Cancel cell phone contracts or put them on hold to the extent possible if the addict will not be using the phone. Most primary treatment centers don't allow cell phone use.

   c. Cancel or negotiate rental agreements and cancel utilities. Clean apartments to protect security deposits or minimize cleaning or damage charges. This one can be therapeutic or overly emotional. If too emotional, or if you don't have the time or energy, this is the first one to skip.

   d. Keep medical insurance in place or get Medicaid, Affordable Care Act or other government benefit programs to cover medical expenses. Drug use may be masking pain that will now return, or the drug use may have created other medical issues that may now need attention, so re-

---

[6] See Chapter 22, Legal Considerations –Estate Planning. Visit www.AddictsMomBook.com for a sample power of attorney document.

taining health insurance, if possible, is beneficial.

Even if it's possible to add your child to your vehicle or health insurance policies, if your child is an adult, policies separate from yours may be preferable. Balance immediate cost savings of adding him/her to your policies vs. potential for increased liability and long term premium increases for you, based on claims because of your child. Separate policies will prevent these claims from impacting your personal policies. These factors are changing constantly with the state of flux of the U.S. health care and overall insurance law, so balancing pros and cons at the time will be important.

e. Close bank accounts to minimize ongoing fees and penalties. Auto-deduct agreements your child may have signed can create ongoing overdrafts, quickly multiplying fees and penalties. Each time an auto-deduct is attempted, new charges can be incurred. Closing the account prevents this.

f. If it's within your budget after a child has entered treatment, retain a good attorney to handle any pending criminal charges. Historically, advice given to parents has been to let legal consequences occur and not to intervene. As an attorney and a Mom, as our current criminal justice system has evolved, I believe this approach has to be reconsidered. Results of criminal charges in today's system can significantly impact your child's long-term options in life, and can compromise steps made in recovery. If this is not financially feasible, it can be very beneficial to work closely with the public defender to provide information and show that family structural and emotional support is there (if it is).[7]

---

[7] See Chapter 24, Legal Considerations - Criminal.

3. **The biggest gray area after the child has entered treatment** is whether to negotiate with creditors to try to put a hold on accumulating interest. Some creditors have hardship provisions, which will hold interest accumulation or significantly reduce interest rates for a period of time to allow a debtor to catch up on the debt. If a creditor is choosing between having to write off the full debt because of a bankruptcy versus structuring a payment plan, many will opt for getting something rather than nothing. Making those calls might make it feasible for the child to repay debt when life is back on track, whereas if interest and penalties accumulate, amounts may get so large that bankruptcy is the only option. If you make these calls, be ready to be pressured by the creditor to pay off principal. Prepare to be strong in sticking only to renegotiating payment plans if that is your goal in making the calls. If the creditor won't agree without principal payment, it's important to be prepared and willing to let go and potentially let a bankruptcy happen. In the big picture, even if bankruptcy results, it's a minor point when compared to death, long term addiction, or prison sentences. Being strong and knowing what you're willing and not willing to do before picking up the phone makes you a better negotiator and keeps these negotiations as unemotional as possible.

We were successful in keeping both of our sons out of bankruptcy, and the negotiations minimized threatening calls from creditors that may have taken focus away from recovery. Keeping them out of bankruptcy also ultimately allowed one of our sons to buy a home when rates and values made home ownership beneficial. He didn't need to obtain a co-signature or to wait until his credit rating was repaired before he could purchase a home or potentially own a business.

Although there are benefits of negotiating with creditors on your child's behalf, it is very stressful and time consuming to sift through the many bills that are typical by the time the addict has hit bottom.

Managing your child's finances when they're working on their recovery should be on the bottom of your list of priorities. Depending on the overall situation, bankruptcy might be the only alternative anyway. Bankruptcy isn't life threatening and creates a credit rating that prevents future credit lines – a good thing in the event of a future relapse. In hindsight, when I think of the hours at my desk trying to get a grip on the financial mess created, a bubble bath may have been more productive, and may have left me in a better emotional state to be supportive of our sons at the time.

In addition to current financial considerations, your estate plan should use trusts so the addict isn't in a position to inherit a lump sum if anything happened to you. It can be very dangerous for an addict actively using or recently out of treatment to experience the loss of one or both parents, and then receive an outright inheritance.[8].

Payments for treatment for your child may be tax deductible to you.[9]

---

[8]   See Chapter 22, Legal Considerations – Estate Planning
[9]   See Chapter 21, Paying for Treatment - Financing and Tax Considerations.

PAYING FOR TREATMENT-
FINANCING AND TAX
CONSIDERATIONS

THE FINAL COST of treatment will vary considerably depending on the level of care and the length of stay. While cost is a huge consideration, cutting costs by shortening stays or ignoring aftercare recommendations may ultimately increase cost for successful treatment in terms of money as well as risk, emotion, and time. Having said that, for many families, self-financing of full treatment simply is not a possibility. Although it's not an easy task, options for financing or coverage for treatment are available.

Many treatment centers have financial counselors who assist with paperwork required for potential insurance coverage, Medicaid eligibility, or scholarship or other programs that aid with cost of care.

Insurance coverage will vary considerably depending on the policy. Many policies have caps on the amount of coverage for mental health related treatment. Coverage may also vary depending on whether services are considered in-network or out-of-network for your specific insurance carrier.

Medicaid or other government programs may cover some of the treatment costs. It is important to review potential Medicaid eligibility and coverage since there are restrictions on how far back Medicaid will cover if an individual isn't Medicaid approved prior to the time services are received.

Provisions of the Affordable Care Act (ACA), a/k/a 'ObamaCare' expand coverage for treatment. Addiction treatment has been categorized as an 'essential health benefit' under the Affordable Care Act which means that most commercial plans will be required to offer coverage. This may not be as positive as it would initially appear, however. An additional five million people may be seeking services, overloading the system, and potentially creating a shortage of available treatment options. Additionally, we have no guarantees that funds will be available to cover the huge cost involved with this expansion of coverage, or that treatment centers will accept the levels of payment offered by the ACA. Providers may simply choose to only accept private pay patients.

For individuals paying for private insurance, premiums may escalate as insurers attempt to recoup the costs they incur in complying with the mandate to cover treatment. Specific application of the new provisions will vary depending on the adoption by each jurisdiction and depending on when treatment is received and the degree to which ACA provisions are implemented and funded.

Because of variations in financial situation, treatment needs, jurisdictional differences in benefits, and costs of treatment, contacting financial counselors supplied by treatment centers is the safest and most efficient method of determining financing options at the time. The cost of treatment can be daunting, but it is worthwhile to research financing options even if you don't believe treatment is affordable. It may be a worthwhile pursuit and can make a huge difference in your child's life as well as your own. Current contact information for treatment centers listed at www.AddictsMomBook.com may be used to locate financial counselors.

U.S. Tax Considerations:

Jurisdictions vary, tax law is constantly in a state of flux, and personal situations impact individual tax considerations. *It's important to see your accountant in regard to your specific planning.* The information here is meant to give an overview of U.S. tax considerations when you are paying for your child's treatment. These rules also apply if you're paying for another relative or member of your household.

For tax returns filed in 2014, if you and your spouse are both under age 65, if you file a U.S. tax return and itemize deductions, you can deduct medical expenses greater than 10% of your adjusted gross income. From Jan. 1, 2013 to Dec. 31, 2016, for individuals 65 and older and their spouses, the medical expense deduction remains at 7.5% of adjusted gross income (which was the % allowable for all ages until 2013.) Amounts paid or reimbursed by insurance or paid from a health savings account (HSA) or covered by a Flexible Savings Account (FSA) won't be included as medical expenses for purposes of the 7.5 or 10% calculation.

The tax code definition of medical expenses specifically includes payments to an inpatient treatment center for alcohol addiction or payments to a therapeutic center for drug addiction. This includes meals and lodging at the center during treatment. Transportation expenses to travel to and from AA meetings, health insurance premiums not paid with pre-tax dollars, and some meals and lodging expenses during travel to and from the center may also be deductible. IRS Publication 502, Medical and Dental Expenses includes detailed descriptions of items that qualify as deductible medical expenses, as well as whose medical expenses you can include as a deduction on your return.

Medical expenses paid for a spouse or a dependent can be deducted even if you can't claim the person as an exemption on your tax return[10]. If you're self-employed, you may deduct up to 100% of your medical insurance costs of a plan established under your business that covers yourself, your spouse, and your dependents. In order

---

[10]   For returns filed in 2014, if you can claim an exemption for a child, you subtract $3,900 for each qualifying child from your adjusted gross income before calculating tax liability. To claim a child as an exemption, the child must live with you more than half the year and be under 19 at the end of the year, or under 24 and a full-time student for the year. If you are subject to the Alternative Minimum Tax, you won't qualify for dependent exemptions.

to meet the definition of dependent for purposes of deductibility, the person receiving the medical services must be a qualifying child or qualifying relative.

If your child is under the age of 19, lives with you, and you're providing over half of his or her support, medical expenses paid will likely be deductible under the qualifying child definition. This definition will also apply if your child is under age 24, is a full-time student, lived with you more than half the year, and did not provide over half of his or her own annual support.

When addiction is an issue, the child may be over age 19 and not be a full time student, or may be over the age of 24. In these cases, the 'qualifying relative' definition may apply to classify your child as a dependent, thereby meeting the requirements for deductibility of medical expenses. Under the tax code, a qualifying relative can include a child (or other relative or member of the household – the code includes an extensive list) who does not meet the requirements of a 'qualifying child' due to age or other factors. A person is a qualifying relative if you provided over half of their support during the subject tax year. *This definition expands the situations in which medical expenses can be deductible.*

To be considered to be your dependent if the person is a qualifying child or qualifying relative, the child must be a U.S. citizen or national, or a resident of the U.S., Canada, or Mexico.

CHAPTER 22

LEGAL CONSIDERATIONS – ESTATE PLANNING

ESTATE PLANNING DOCUMENTS for parents and for adult children can simplify management of finances and medical care, allow the parent to obtain important information, and protect assets for the benefit of all beneficiaries. Documents signed by your adult children, as well as documents for your own estate plan can save money, protect family relationships, maintain privacy, and minimize cost, delays and frustrations of paperwork. To legally execute documents, your son or daughter must be over the age of eighteen, must be mentally competent and must sign documents voluntarily. These documents are beneficial regardless of whether addiction is an issue or not. It's a good idea, when your child reaches age 18, to put documents in place.

DOCUMENT OPTIONS FOR YOUR CHILDREN:

Durable Financial Power of Attorney: This document authorizes another person to act (the agent) in place of the principal (the person signing the document). If your son or daughter signed a power of attorney authorizing you to act on his or her behalf, you would be the agent. A specific power of attorney can authorize only limited powers, or a broader power of attorney can basically allow the agent to handle any financial affairs that the principal would handle on his or her own.

Making the power of attorney 'durable' means that it remains in effect if the principal becomes incompetent. If the document doesn't specifically state something like "This Power of Attorney shall not be affected by my subsequent disability, incapacity, or incompetency", by law, it will expire if incapacity occurs.

Having a power of attorney can be imperative if you want to assess your child's financial situation, negotiate with creditors, or sign financial documents on your child's behalf.

Most states have statutory powers of attorney based on state statute. The state form or a more generic form may be used.[11]

Living Will/Durable Health Care Power of Attorney: These documents authorize the appointed agent to make health care decisions on the principal's behalf if the principal is unable to make decisions. These documents also authorize decisions to be made in regard to continuation of life support systems, and also admission to a nursing home. In many states, a standard Power of Attorney for Health Care document is designated by statute and may be obtained from your attorney or your physician. If no document is signed to authorize you to access medical records or to make medical decisions, a full court proceeding could be required before you would be able to access medical information. It's important to use the Health Care form applicable to your specific jurisdiction. Health care providers and their attorneys will be accustomed to seeing the statutory form for your jurisdiction, so will more readily accept that form.

HIPAA: The Health Insurance Portability and Accountability Act of 1996 was passed to protect the privacy of an individual's health information. Without a signed HIPAA release form, if your adult child ends up in the hospital, medical personnel will not be able to release medical information to you. Having this document signed provides authorization to obtain those records.[12]

---

[11]   Visit www.AddictsMomBook.com for a sample Durable Financial Power of Attorney.
[12]   Visit www.AddictsMomBook.com for a sample HIPAA form.

Authorization for Release of Information: This form authorizes third parties to release information to you. Without this document, third parties could create liability for themselves if they released your adult child's information to you. This authorization specifically authorizes them to provide information to you, and protects them from potential liability for doing so. This is a broad authorization for release of information, which could be used to obtain information from educational institutions, treatment centers or others who may have important information.[13]

While it is possible that individual institutions may require their own forms to be used, having all of the documents above executed by your child gives you options and increases the chances that you will be able to access information when needed.

DOCUMENT OPTIONS FOR PARENTS:

In addition to having the documents described above signed by your adult child so you can act on his or her behalf, it is also a good idea for you to sign those same documents to appoint someone who can act on your behalf if needed. All of the documents described above are effective during the lifetime of the principal signing the document.

Additionally, documents should be put in place to designate management and distribution of assets in the event of your death. This is particularly important when addiction is an issue in the family. Providing for management of assets protects property, provides financial security for family members, and eliminates the risk that inheriting a sum of money outright could jeopardize the addict's sobriety.

Wills and living trusts are both used to designate beneficiaries to inherit assets. When addiction is present in the family, the privacy that may be maintained with a living trust can be beneficial. This can prevent an active addict from seeing the inventory of assets (which is public if a will is administered in probate court), and prevents terms of asset management from being public information. A will must go

---

[13]   Visit www.AddictsMomBook.com for sample Authorization for Release of Information.

through the probate process, whereas a living trust authorizes the trustee you appoint to pay bills, handle final paperwork, and distribute assets according to the plan of distribution in the trust without going through the probate process.

As part of the plan of distribution whether a will or a living trust is used, a testamentary trust (which comes into being after death) can set up management of assets for a beneficiary in lieu of distributing assets outright to that individual. When addiction is involved or if a potential beneficiary doesn't have money management abilities, coming into a lump sum at the same time the addict has just lost a parent can create a high-risk situation. Trust provisions may be adapted to fit the individual situation and set appropriate timelines and management specifications for your family.

If a beneficiary is or may be the recipient of government benefits that could be jeopardized if an inheritance was received, the inheritance may be placed in a special needs trust with specific restrictions on management of assets to benefit the beneficiary without jeopardizing government benefits. The provisions of the special needs trust should be carefully drafted to meet the requirements of your jurisdiction and to achieve your individual goals.

Additionally, if an adult child is residing with you and would need a place to live for a period of time in the event of your death, estate planning documents may provide for a life estate, or the right to reside in the home for a limited period of time. If these provisions are included in your estate plan, make sure the document also specifies who would pay expenses for the property during that period of occupancy. If the life estate could jeopardize government benefits, putting restrictions on the term of occupancy can protect that eligibility for those benefits.

It's essential that estate plans be drafted to achieve your specific goals, taking the facts of your individual situation into consideration. While it's easy to put this low on the priority list when dealing with all of the other effects of addiction, estate planning can make a tremendous difference and is well worth the effort.

CHAPTER **23**

NEGOTIATING A CONTRACT WITH TEEN OR ADULT CHILD LIVING AT HOME

WHEN A CHILD with a history of chemical dependency is living at home, having a written contract can avoid misunderstandings and future conflict. The best thing about any contract is that it gives an objective reason for both parties to discuss what they want, and what they don't want. This is much easier to do before issues come up, when discussions can be less emotional. Ideally, if your child is not currently living with you, the discussion and the contract should be completed prior to the time the child returns home.

The worst thing about any contract is if one party knows the other party won't enforce it. So, in creating a contract for a child living at home or returning home, a good agreement is one that:

1. Is concise enough to be clear and easy for all parties to be aware if a provision isn't being met.
2. Includes the major items that each party wants and doesn't want.
3. Has benefits for each party if the contract terms are followed.
4. Has objective consequences if terms are not followed.

    5.   Only lists consequences that will actually be objectively measured and enforced.

The greatest benefit from the contract is the communication required to put it in place. Simply copying someone else's contract verbatim misses the point. However, it's always easier to edit than to draft from scratch, and it's helpful to know what's worked for other people – so drafts to use as a starting point are available at www.AddictsMomBook.com.

Sitting down and discussing what each of you envisions can set a foundation that makes the difference between a relaxed relationship and domestic war. Your family has gone through immense change. Even in the best of situations, this can create some conflict. Expect it. When it happens, though, it's helpful to have a framework based on up-front discussions and a written agreement.

Compliance with any agreement will be greatest if all parties have an active part in determining contract provisions. If your child has been in treatment, your child's counselor can be an excellent moderator for discussions and creation of a contract. A counselor can make sure that each person is given an opportunity for input, and will keep the discussion on track.

Here are some discussion points that can help to create a framework for your agreement, along with some typical responses from parents and recovering addicts.

1. What is your greatest fear in regard to this living arrangement?

Parent: e.g., Relapse and continued use of drugs.

Child: e.g., Relapse, disappointing my parents (S/he may not admit this one up front but it's often a factor.)

In a black and white world, it would be easy to have a contract that simply says, "If you use drugs, you must move out." If you would enforce that, it may be a logical contract provision. If you know you would *not* do that, then don't put it in the contract or all terms will be meaningless. In our agreement, we didn't require an immediate move following a relapse. We gave ourselves the discretion to require a move if drug use continued or if behavior in the home was unacceptable or significantly disrupted life in our home. In some cases, allowing an addict who's relapsed to continue living in the home can provide a foundation on which to rebuild, to apply what was learned in treatment, and to get back on track. This does not mean there would be no consequences, or that parents should accept *continued* drug use or having an active addict in their home.

The best contract terms will be very different from family to family depending upon age, individual personalities, response to treatment, whether there are other children in the home who could be impacted, and other overall family and living circumstances.

3. **How could we best minimize our fears?**

Parent: e.g., Identify situations that we believe could increase the risk of relapse and have assurances from you that you'll stay away from those situations.

Child: e.g., Having a sobriety plan to follow and knowing that if I follow it, my parents will trust me.

3. **What is most likely to irritate you?**

Parent: e.g., Extensive time laying on the couch in inactivity, loud rap music, not cleaning up after yourself, not pursuing work, school, or other productive activities.

Child: e.g., Being micro-managed; not having any privacy

Discussion on this issue shouldn't be a laundry list of anything that's ever been irritating, but it is important to acknowledge those things that'll likely get under your skin. I wanted to appreciate our sons' music so when rap was played in our home, I initially tried to hold it in. The result was that I became irritable and less tolerant of everyone and everything. Ultimately, just admitting that I didn't want to hear it was preferable for everyone over not being up front about it and letting it impact my state of mind.

Completing a treatment program significantly changes our children. It was sometimes difficult for me to acknowledge that they'd developed and had survived without my daily contact. The more I pushed, the more they resisted. If your son or daughter is maintaining sobriety and living a successful life, micro-management and restricting privacy can be counter-productive.

4. **What do you appreciate most about the progress your son or daughter has made so far, or what do you appreciate most about your parent(s)?**

Parent: Be specific about details you've noticed, showing you're in touch with his or her accomplishments and growth and truly appreciate all of the effort and the successes.

Child: Example, but one you might not hear right away – I'm grateful for my Mom and/or Dad's support through everything I've put them through, and their willingness to let me come home.

Including this question in the discussion gives an opportunity to be positive, and reminds us that living together could be an opportunity to rebuild relationships and to have fun seeing one another on a daily basis without the barriers and challenges that active addiction previously created. If your child is light on praise at this point, don't feel badly and don't let it derail contract negotiations. If they stay on the path of sobriety, there'll come a time when you'll hear appreciation.

I sometimes forgot how much progress had been made. I avoided thinking back to the active addiction days, but periodically needed to do that to appreciate how far we'd all come.

Learning to be Mom to sober, independent sons was a transition for me. Part of my difficulty was the change in role and figuring out where I belonged in their lives. The other part was legitimate concern and self-preservation. It took time to have faith that they wouldn't relapse or fall into old patterns (or that even if they might, my micro-managing wouldn't prevent it). Addiction thwarts the maturity process, so even after treatment, there were times that our sons continued to act immaturely, but my hovering only irritated them. It did not help in expediting their maturity. The maturation process that's slowed during active addiction does catch up with time.

As I finally began to let go, our relationships improved. As I let go of my baggage, it was easier for our sons to pick up responsibility for their own lives. I still work on this, but being conscious of it has been beneficial for me, and I'm now thoroughly enjoying my newfound freedom.

5. **Describe your vision of what success under this agreement would look like.**

Parent: e.g. - Having some family meals together; having some positive family time; parents and child having freedom to live their own lives and have personal time not involving the other.

Child: e.g. – Having a place to live while having some independence; being able to get back on my feet, work my program, and save some money without unsolicited input from my parents.

It's difficult for contract provisions to create success if the vision for success for each party is totally different, especially if parties don't realize that their visions are different. It's not necessary to completely agree on the desired outcome, but discussing and being aware of what each envisions can be enlightening, and help each party to understand goals and motivations of the other.

6. What will each party be responsible for paying or contributing?

Parent: e.g., After _____, we will expect rent in the amount of _____ OR We won't expect rent, and will cover costs of (e.g. - health and car insurance) for _____ months. We will expect _____ (amount of payment toward anything in particular, or in addition to or in lieu of payment, specific areas of responsibility).

Child: e.g., I will pay for _____ and help with _____.

This will obviously depend heavily on the age of the child and financial situation of parents and child. However, even if parents can afford to cover all costs, doing so deprives your son or daughter of the sense of satisfaction that comes with being self-supporting and productive. This *is* enabling. If the parents are in a financial position to help *and* if helping with finances for a short time allows for job hunting, finishing education, or other situations where the child is being productive and working toward self-sufficiency, then it may make sense to subsidize. If this is the case, time limits and objective measurements should be put in place so it doesn't turn into a long-term support situation.

7. Initial term of this contract (target date for re-negotiation or target date for child to move out on his/her own)

Parent: e.g., Within a year, but before you move out, you must be totally self-supporting. If you choose to move out before you're self-supporting, any subsidies from us will stop immediately. We don't want to be paying your car and health insurance premiums and have your money going to pay rent rather than covering all of your costs.

Child: e.g., 2 months – as soon as I can save a security deposit

A lot can happen, and a specific move-out date may not be practical, but at a minimum, a specific date should be set to review the agreement, discuss terms and make any adjustments.

CHAPTER 24

LEGAL CONSIDERATIONS – CRIMINAL

CONVENTIONAL WISDOM HAS been to allow the addict to suffer the consequences of their actions, including criminal charges and ramifications. Theoretically, I agree. The reality, however, is that our criminal justice system is so broken that it can ruin your child's life on a permanent basis without achieving benefits. It's inconsistent, disorganized, and in serious need of change to protect the public as well as the taxpayer. The experiences with our sons filled a huge gap in my knowledge of criminal law. Until our family experienced this system on a personal basis, I knew there were some issues but also believed that for the most part, the system protected the public and punished criminals appropriately. Those beliefs changed completely with personal experience.

The best advice for everyone is to do everything possible to stay out of the system. It's broken, it's dangerous, and it's important to avoid it. Unfortunately, when addiction is involved logical advice is seldom heeded and criminal issues are typical.

As an attorney, although my focus is not in the area of criminal law, being able to research and review the law gave me some insight into what was happening, when it made sense, and when it was a system completely out of control. I believe most of those administering the system are well meaning, but each person is a small cog in a huge wheel and few see the actual outcomes of the overall system or have the power to do anything about it. We experienced the system firsthand and it wasn't pretty, even though we were able to keep our sons from felony convictions or long term jail or prison time. Many aren't as fortunate.

Having legal representation is essential. *Specific questions should be directed to a criminal attorney.* However, it is helpful to have an overview of what you're dealing with in regard to criminal law, so here are some basics.

Criminal charges may be federal or state. On the first page of the criminal complaint, if the top says 'U.S. District Court' it's a federal charge. The first page of the complaint in a state charge will say something like "X County District Court". Drug offenses may be prosecuted under either state or federal law. The prosecutor is the sole decision maker as to where the case will be filed.

The complaint will also cite the law under which charges are being filed, as well as a description of the alleged violation. For a parent, it takes a strong stomach to read the charges. Details may be included that you'd rather not see, and the outline of potential penalties in the complaint or within the cited statute can send chills up the back of any Mom or Dad. It is important to take charges very seriously and to get the best representation possible. Typically maximum penalties are not served and often plea agreements can be negotiated to avoid prison, particularly on first offenses, but beneficial outcomes should never be assumed.

The most dangerous and frightening aspects of criminal law are federal and state mandatory minimum statutes and state three-strikes statutes. These laws can have devastating consequences and leave judges with absolutely no discretion in sentencing. In numerous cases, court transcripts show judges apologizing and frustrated that the law mandates that they apply penalties that far exceed what the judge believes is appropriate. Section 21 of the U.S. Code, section 841 contains mandatory minimum sentences ranging from five years to life in prison without release. Prior felonies or more than one felony charge in the same arrest may increase minimum penalties to ten or twenty years.

Unfortunately, rather than getting drug kingpins off the streets, many addicts and low-level, non-violent offenders are caught by the provisions of these statutes and serve inordinately long sentences for their levels of involvement. These defendants often have no information to exchange for special consideration by prosecutors who decide what charges are to be filed, so are in a disadvantageous negotiating position. Dual diagnosis addicts with poor communication skills are at a particular disadvantage.

Twenty-four states[14] still have three strikes laws where severe mandatory minimum sentences apply after three convictions. In 2003, the U.S. Supreme Court upheld three strikes laws by a 5-4 majority, saying they do not violate the eighth amendment 'cruel and unusual punishment' provision of the U.S. Constitution. However, in recent years the trend has been to reduce mandatory minimums under these statutes and to increase judges' discretion in sentencing. Reforms have occurred based on the devastating effects, not only for the prisoners but also for the taxpayers who have carried the burden of the huge expense of long-term incarcerations. Families Against Mandatory Minimums (www.FAMM.org) has excellent, current information on each state's statutes as well as federal law and recent legal developments.

At one time, I assumed that marijuana offenses would not result in severe criminal penalties. After all, as of 2013, two states (Washington and Colorado) and some individual cities in Maine and Michigan have legalized pot and movements appear to be moving toward more

---

[14]　The 24 states that have three strikes laws are: Arkansas, California, Colorado, Connecticut, Florida, Georgia, Indiana, Kansas, Louisiana, Maryland, Montana, Nevada, New Jersey, New Mexico, North Carolina, North Dakota, Pennsylvania, South Carolina, Tennessee, Utah, Vermont, Virginia, Washington, and Wisconsin.

recreational use legalization. Twenty states[15] plus Washington D.C. have medical marijuana statutes. Unfortunately, even in those states, federal prosecution can still be pursued since federal law takes precedence over state law. State or federal prosecutions can alter lives through severe prison sentences and felony convictions. Additionally, felony drug convictions bar students from receiving federal student loans, essentially freezing these students out of opportunities to finance higher education.

According to the FBI's Uniform Crime Reporting data, in 2011 49.5% of all drug arrests were for marijuana. Just under 70% of all federal marijuana offenders sentenced had very few or no prior convictions. Thirty-five states[16] use imprisonment for simple possession of marijuana and sentences vary significantly.

Driver's licenses are used like weapons even when the offense has nothing to do with driving. The propensity of the criminal justice system to suspend driver's licenses for many infractions that are totally unrelated to vehicles leaves many with the option of not getting to work or driving without a license. In many cases, licenses are suspended with no notice provided, or with notice several months later. In these instances, if an accident occurs, insurance may be compromised even if the insured had no notice that the license had been suspended. If another offense occurred, even if the driver was unaware of the revocation, driving without a license can trigger much more severe penalties.

The sixth amendment to the Constitution provides that in "all criminal prosecutions, the accused shall enjoy the right to a speedy and public trial. . . " While it's true that technically, a defendant can demand a

---

[15]   The 20 states which currently have medical marijuana laws are Alaska, Arizona, California, Colorado, Connecticut, Delaware, Hawaii, Illinois, Maine, Massachusetts, Michigan, Montana, New Hampshire, Nevada, New Jersey, New Mexico, Oregon, Rhode island, Vermont and Washington. Washington D.C. also authorizes medical marijuana. At this time, 15 additional states have medical marijuana legislation pending. This is a constantly developing area of the law.

[16]   The 15 states that do NOT use imprisonment to punish at least some types of simple marijuana possession are Alaska, California, Colorado, Connecticut, Maine, Massachusetts, Minnesota, Mississippi, Nebraska, Nevada, New York, North Carolina, Ohio, Oregon and Washington.

speedy trial, in practice, prompt resolution of cases is a fallacy.

Maximum penalties for many drug-related offenses include felony charges and jail time. Often, this can be pled to misdemeanors with probation or other lesser penalties not involving incarceration. The challenge is that, if the prosecutor chooses to delay by simply ignoring the case or not agreeing to discuss a reasonable plea agreement, defendants and their attorneys are hesitant to push the prosecutor since delay is typically better than jail time. It can also be risky to irritate or alienate the prosecutor since s/he has an enormous amount of discretion in resolution of the case, and having to proceed to a trial can be extremely expensive, emotional and time consuming, and results are difficult to predict.

On a practical level, prosecutors can take whatever time they choose, with the defendant having to appear in court regularly just for the case to *again* be moved forward and yet another hearing date to be scheduled. This wastes taxpayer money, increases legal fees, raises havoc with scheduling if the defendant is working, and often makes the defendant unable to find work if unemployed. What employer wants to hire someone who needs time off for court on an ongoing basis, or who could end up in jail? There are laws that prohibit discrimination against those who are being prosecuted, but it's hard to blame an employer for finding reasons to substantiate not making this hire, and there are many subjective reasons for an employer to show why one candidate is hired over another. The Internet leaves permanent, easy-to-access records that follow defendants forever. The charges, whether eventually ending in convictions or not, continue to be listed in the public record except in some cases of minor defendants or unless special agreements for record expungement are entered into.

The fifth and fourteenth amendments require 'due process of law', including the right to cross-examine, to apply the rules of evidence, and the right to a jury trial. Again, while it's true that, technically, these rights are available, in actual practice, most cases don't go to trial so these protections mean little. Prosecutors are given 'prosecutorial discretion', with few restrictions at the stage where they decide to bring charges. Multiple charges are often listed. A defendant, arrested for possession of one substance, may end up being charged with several different counts for that one substance, and charges may be a laundry list of offenses that may, or may not, have occurred.

I witnessed an example of this type of prosecution. Police arrived at a home with a warrant for the individual who resided there. Another person was visiting. The visitor was arrested, and ultimately charged with multiple counts based on a bottle of Percocet and a small quantity of pot. Charges included possession of Methamphetamine, which the defendant claimed he did not have. In reviewing the evidence, the defense attorney could find no trace of Meth. The prosecutor's answer: There was only enough on the outside of the bottle to be tested. The fact that there was no longer any trace left did not impact the charges filed. This reference to Meth significantly increased the risk if the defendant went to trial. Although this charge would likely not be provable at trial, having that charge appear could taint a jury. Unfortunately, juries tend to believe that if a charge is included there must have been a reason for it, so even if there's no conviction on that charge, chances of conviction on other counts likely increase.

This defendant eventually entered into a plea, accepting seven misdemeanor counts. The charge of possession of meth on the record will likely impact decisions made by the probation officer. The meth charge will also permanently be on the record, to be seen by potential employers and anyone else who accesses the Internet.

The irony of this particular case was that appearances in the process of negotiations were delayed because one of the attorneys in the case had been in a car accident and was on pain medication – which happened to be Percocet – the exact same drug for which the defendant was being prosecuted. The defendant had significant pain issues and did not have a prescription because physicians were afraid to write one.

In application, prosecutors and probation agents have much more power in our current criminal justice system than the courts, and there are few practical protections for the accused within this system. Resolution of criminal cases and the lives of those prosecuted is largely based on subjective decisions of prosecutors at the point that charges are filed and subjective decisions by probation officers in controlling the lives of the 'offenders' assigned to them.

Legal Representation:

The sixth amendment guarantees every person accused of a crime to counsel. If convicted, a defendant has the right to one appeal and counsel for representation on that appeal. Public defenders or court appointed attorneys are made available to defendants who cannot afford a private attorney. Public defenders are full time government employees, whereas court-appointed attorneys are private attorneys paid by the government to handle individual cases. Which will apply will depend on the jurisdiction, the type of case, the overall work load at the time, and whether conflicts of interest are present if the public defender handles the case. Although the law requires that representation be provided, there is no right to select a specific attorney. Public defenders are very familiar with the criminal court system, but if you're not happy with the assigned attorney there's no right to a reassignment.

If you don't qualify for a public defender or a court-appointed attorney or choose to retain a private attorney, payment may be based on hourly billing or a flat fee. Flat fees typically have a cap on the maximum number of hours that will be covered by the retainer, or are limited to pre-trial negotiations with an additional retainer required if the matter goes to trial. Criminal cases do not use contingency billing where the attorney is paid based on the outcome of the case.

Keep in mind that the attorney represents the defendant – not the parents – even if you're paying the bill. The attorney may provide you with information only if your son or daughter authorizes sharing of information. Attorneys' approaches vary significantly in regard to communication and relationships with parents. It's your child's attorney, but if you're paying the bill, you have the right to select which attorney to retain.

It is essential to interview attorneys prior to selecting one. We learned this the hard way, as discussed below. This is an extremely stressful time of life. Having the most possible confidence in the attorney and having a good working relationship with him or her can be the difference between insomnia and at least some nights of decent sleep.

It is important to be respectful of the attorney's time, to be succinct and efficient with your questions, and to organize information that could be helpful to the attorney in presenting your child's case. Most criminal attorneys are caring individuals who want to help, but this is their business. In the initial interview, if you are disorganized or require a long period of time, the retainer may increase. The attorney's asset is his or her time and if it appears that you'll be high maintenance, that risk will generally be calculated into the quote. Also, the best criminal attorneys have more business than they can handle. As parents, we want this to be the most important case for the attorney. That's simply too much to ask, but it's not too much to expect the attorney to be well prepared, to know the facts of the case, and to keep the client informed.

Our Personal Experience:

Politicians and bureaucrats often look at criminal law broadly. Theoretically, statutes and accompanying processes and regulations may make sense. However, to assess the success or failure of any legislation, the actual impact and results must be understood. Sharing the details of our personal experiences with the criminal justice system may help parents in making decisions on the degree of help to provide. Hopefully, the story of our experiences can also give those working in the criminal justice system, as well as politicians promoting and passing criminal law, some insight into the actual application of these laws on real peoples' lives.

Involvement of parents can be essential to preventing their child from becoming a statistic of our criminal justice system. Children are lost to the system daily, with felony convictions and prison sentences for non-violent drug crimes severely restricting future opportunities. As parents, we can be torn between wanting to help and hesitating because we've heard that we shouldn't enable and should allow our child to feel the consequences of his or her actions. This is appropriate if the criminal activity has included violence or if your child is unwilling to get help with the addiction. In that case, jail is preferable to continued, untreated use. If you are able to get your child into treatment in lieu of incarceration, based on our experience, it is definitely worth doing what you can to facilitate that.

Our sons fared better than many, escaping extended jail time or felony convictions. Despite that, the stress, expense and overall saga of dealing with the criminal justice system would have been incomprehensible to me before our personal experience. I'll outline details of just one of the prosecutions to shed light on the impact of this system on families. Had this been a unique experience, I wouldn't include it here. Unfortunately, this is indicative of how the system really works. Details may vary from case to case, but the risks, bureaucracy, stress and financial burdens are the same.

Ben was arrested in Arizona two days before he got on the plane to be admitted to the 28-day inpatient treatment program. He was not charged at that time. Since he had left the state, I was concerned that a warrant could be issued for his arrest and that he could end up with bigger legal issues if he wasn't aware if charges were filed. Ben formally changed his mailing address to our home address so no mail would be missed and a valid address would be on the public record. I attempted to search Arizona records, but wasn't certain I'd pick up a filed charge, so we contacted a law firm in Arizona to run a monthly check to make sure nothing was filed. After a year, there was no activity so we quit checking.

Fifteen months passed after the arrest. Ben had completed both primary treatment and his 5 ½ months of aftercare, had been drug and alcohol free for two days short of fifteen months, and was now working as sous chef for Gray Wolf and setting an example for young men entering the program. At that time, he received a call from friends in

Arizona telling him that a police SWAT team had stormed their apartment looking for Ben, with a warrant for his arrest.

Ben's address change to our house was public knowledge, yet no notice was sent. After fifteen months of inactivity, the justice system decided there was so much urgency to find Ben that they went through the effort to get a no-knock warrant to enter this apartment rather than checking with the post office or just searching online for his very public address. This intrusion into innocent peoples' lives and the cost of sending out a SWAT team could have been averted with a simple check of public records for Ben's current address or mailing of a warrant to his old address for forwarding to him. Ah, tax dollars at work!

One of the arguments for criminal sanctions is to protect the public. This is a noble and rational goal. If the criminal justice system is based on believing that the offender poses a threat to the public (which may be a logical assumption when an addict is actively using), isn't it important to file charges during that time period when the offender poses the greatest threat to the public? Protection of the public is obviously not achieved if the system has no knowledge of the offender's whereabouts for more than a year following the arrest. The system had NO idea what our son was doing for those fifteen months. Any goal of protecting the public was obviously not achieved. So, the result is the worst of all worlds. The public is not protected and taxpayer money is spent in pursuing the offender after an extended time period.

Another goal of criminal law is to prevent future criminal activity. In our son's case, filing charges after he'd dedicated the preceding fifteen months to turning his life around was poor timing. If charges had been filed at the time of the arrest and he'd negotiated a deferred prosecution, he would have been aware that charges were pending and the steps he had taken would have fully satisfied court requirements. By the time the prosecutor decided to pursue this case, Ben believed his past life was behind him. At the time he was treasuring success, this was a huge setback and felt like punishment for voluntarily doing all the right things.

In many states, charges may be filed up to six years (and in some cases even longer time periods) after an offense has taken place. This could be logical if the alleged criminal was hiding and couldn't be located or if new evidence was discovered, but when peoples' lives are on hold because a bureaucracy may not get around to filing charges until up to six years after an incident, the results are destructive and counter-productive. Late filing of charges may be based on inefficiencies in the system, or may be politically motivated by a prosecutor who, for any number of reasons, wants to be perceived as 'tough on crime'.

When Ben heard about this incident at his former apartment, he immediately contacted us and we contacted the Arizona attorney to check the record. Charges had indeed been filed. We retained the attorney to contact the court and notify them that Ben would voluntarily appear.

One of the charges filed in Ben's case was a DUI. Driving under the influence is a serious offense. If he was impaired behind the wheel, he was risking other people's lives as well as his own. Prosecution was warranted, but a delay of over a year did NOT protect the public. While this old charge was being pursued, immediate cases were likely not being processed, continuing to exacerbate the problem and leaving individuals with current drug and alcohol issues behind the wheel.

I researched the law and reviewed the statute. This charge was a misdemeanor with a one-year statute of limitations with some exceptions. One of the exceptions was if the offender was driving on a suspended license. In that case, a DUI is a felony with a seven-year statute of limitations. On its face, this rule makes sense. We want to discourage driving without a license and certainly want to discourage driving under the influence without a license. The issue is that driver's licenses are revoked for numerous reasons including unpaid parking tickets, and in many cases no notice of revocation is given until months after the revocation applies. In Ben's case, he had some unpaid parking tickets. I was aware of potential ramifications of not paying these tickets (license revocation, insurance premium increases or unavailability of coverage, etc.), so we helped him with these tickets a few months prior to his arrest. This could be enabling, but we considered this expense in a category similar to paying insurance premiums. Covering a small expense now could prevent a much larger expense later.

If we hadn't helped to pay those parking tickets, under the statute, when charges were filed fifteen months later, he would have fallen under a **mandatory felony conviction and a four-month minimum prison sentence**. For Ben, those paid parking tickets were the difference between going directly to jail or having that charge dropped because the statute of limitations had expired. I can only imagine how destructive a four-month prison sentence could have been at that time. We'd invested enormous energy and money in all the treatment he'd received, and he'd poured his heart and soul into recovery. A prison sentence at that point would have been an enormous setback.

Is this a system you want applied to your child? We decided to do what we could to keep our kids out of the system through treatment so they could make better decisions. We'll help to minimize the damage the system can inflict through the best attorneys we can afford and by being actively involved with watching what's going on with the case.

It seems that we should be on the same side as the criminal justice system. There should be a common goal for all of our children to be contributing members of society. We'd taken every possible step to promote that since Ben's arrest, and he'd thrown himself into work toward that goal as well. Now, we had to focus more energy and money to fight the system so it didn't undo the progress he'd made. Ben's focus on working at the treatment center, serving as an example to young men just entering the program, now shifted to hiring attorneys and worrying about going to prison.

Hiring an attorney doesn't solve all the issues either. Because of the distance involved and because his office had checked records for us over a period of time, we did not meet with the Arizona attorney prior to retaining him in Ben's case, nor did we have a phone conversation of any substance. We ended up regretting that.

Following our notice that charges had been filed, our first trip to Phoenix was for the arraignment where Ben was to be formally charged and the warrant for his arrest was to be dropped. We decided to meet Ben in Phoenix so we could meet the attorney and be there to support our son. Until the court ordered otherwise, technically the warrant for his arrest was still in place so we wanted to be there in case he ran into trouble. It would also be nice to spend some time with Ben, even under these circumstances. He flew from Washington State, and we flew from Minneapolis.

I'd spoken to the attorney beforehand and asked if he could take steps to minimize the number of trips to Arizona that would be required. I asked if records from the treatment centers or any other information would be helpful and he said they would be, so we gathered that information and sent it to him several days prior to the hearing date.

The night before we flew to Arizona I laid awake hoping that this would be our last trip and our last sleepless night wondering whether one of our sons would end up in jail. We hoped for a life in the future without these types of concerns looming.

The morning we were all to fly to Arizona, I considered calling to make sure Ben left for the plane on time, but then remembered that he's now responsible and needs no reminders. When I received a message that our flight was delayed, I called to let him know, and he was going through security – two hours before his flight just to make sure there were no issues. Our son had become a mature, caring, responsible adult.

Unfortunately, the arrest just before he entered treatment had put him into the system, and I prayed that we could extract him. At that point based on everything he'd done to turn his life around, we were certain that the best outcome for everyone would be for charges to be dropped, but we were at the mercy of the prosecutor and the criminal attorney we'd hired.

I researched the attorney. He's supposed to be the best. The retainer will be worth the pain if he gets the results we need. We'll never know if we could have had similar or better results with less expensive counsel, the public defender, or negotiating with the prosecutor myself, but we didn't feel that this was a time to take risks.

Our highly credentialed attorney has, for the most part, completely ignored us. He hasn't instilled confidence, but changing counsel in the middle of this process could hurt us, and hopefully we'll see his expertise in negotiations tomorrow. Knowing the local system and the players within it can make a big difference in the outcome.

We were understandably nervous as we entered the courthouse. Even for me, the courthouse atmosphere was intimidating and entering with Ben, knowing the outstanding warrant for his arrest was still in place put me in a state of fear and gave me empathy for how he must have been feeling.

My first impression of the attorney when we were in Arizona was not positive. We were told to meet him in the courthouse cafeteria at 8:30 for an 8:30 hearing. We arrived at 8:15 and called his office at 8:50 to determine whether we were missing the hearing. The office said he was on his way.

At 9:15, the attorney finally walked into the cafeteria, came up to our table, introduced himself, made no explanation for his delay, and left, wandering to other tables and ultimately sitting at a table directly beside us, chatting and making small talk with another attorney. I approached him and asked that he give us an overview of the morning.

I'd sent an email to the attorney providing a summary of all Ben had done since his arrest, records from the treatment centers, as well as a statement of our support and observations. Michael's attorney had requested these types of statements when he went through criminal proceedings, and the court in his case had ultimately commented that those facts and supportive family did impact their decision. It quickly became obvious that the attorney had no concept of Ben's situation – he hadn't read the email. He also had no paperwork, saying the Public Defender's office had it and had not yet given it to him.

Clearly, my requests to have as much done as possible to minimize future trips had fallen on deaf ears.

When Ben's case was finally called, the judge asked if the attorney had the paperwork. It became clear that, had this attorney been on top of things, much more could have been resolved today. After watching several cases prior to Ben's appearance, it was also obvious that today's judge was one we would want to be in front of for resolution. Our attorney was only there for the formality of quashing the warrant for Ben's arrest. When the judge began talking about whether the court should mandate drug testing, I nearly came out of my chair since the attorney made no mention of Ben's long term successful treatment and that he now WORKS at the treatment center. Court mandated testing adds ongoing cost and requires trips to testing locations, which can interfere with a job. Testing at the center where Ben worked was prohibited by the organization administering the court mandates.

These tests may be appropriate in the case of someone who's been picked up on drug charges recently or hasn't undergone any treatment, but that mandate no longer fits Ben's situation. Finally, the judge asked where Ben was living and why he'd left the state, and Ben explained the circumstances. The warrant was quashed and paperwork was provided to the attorney. A return court date was scheduled, requiring another trip to Phoenix. More time and money.

The attorney's office had told us, for purposes of scheduling flights, we'd certainly be done with everything by noon. To be cautious, our flights were at 3:30. At the conclusion of the hearing, the attorney handed us paperwork and directed us to go to downtown Phoenix so Ben could be fingerprinted. We proceeded downtown to find a sign notifying us that the wait may be 4-5 hours. I went to the desk and explained our situation, to be told we just needed to take the ticket, sit down and wait. Others in the waiting area heard our plight and assured us that things were moving faster than the sign indicated, and that an hour should do it. We relaxed a bit. Hopefully, we'd make our flights.

At that time, three police officers came up and surrounded Ben saying there was a warrant for his arrest. We explained that the warrant was quashed, and that the attorney had given us the paperwork to come here after the warrant had been quashed. They responded that the paperwork did not show that, but that they would go to check. The officers returned, proceeded with fingerprinting, and let us go. Apparently, they'd checked with the court to update the paperwork. I became more and more frustrated with the attorney, and I was very thankful that we'd accompanied Ben to Phoenix. Although at this point Ben could have handled this, our age, experience and support decreased the chances of an inadvertent fiasco and made this process less frightening for him. Our presence may have minimized the issue with the police who were attempting to arrest Ben on the warrant. The experiences on this trip also put us on notice that we couldn't trust this attorney to be on top of things or to be protective of Ben. We proceeded to the airport and headed home.

The attorney assured me that he would have paperwork on the case within the week and would contact us with his analysis of the severity of the charges and a plan of action. We heard nothing for several months, and our calls were screened. Finally, I called and demanded that a phone conference be scheduled.

Three days later, I spoke with the attorney. I've read the statutes and the charges so have a general idea of what we're dealing with, but hope he can give a specific overview of our options. The phone conversation is short, it's obvious that he hasn't allocated time for the call, and he isn't prepared. An obvious issue I've spotted is a one-year statute of limitations on the DUI charge. He doesn't mention it. When I bring it up, his response is "Well, there you go!"

Based on my specific request, the attorney promised that he would begin negotiations with the prosecutor to attempt to get this resolved on our next visit so we wouldn't have to continue making trips. I hoped that he could give us some idea of our risks and some guidance as to probable outcome of the case. That could have relieved some of the worry. We received none of that. Going for months, waiting to learn whether Ben could end up in jail or with a felony conviction was excruciating for him and for us. The attorney and those administering the system were either oblivious to this or simply didn't care.

The next hearing was on a Monday. On the Thursday before, I had still heard nothing from the attorney. I called his office and again couldn't reach him. I was told he would return my call. Mid-afternoon on Friday I called him and told the assistant it was imperative that I speak with him, as we would be boarding a plane over the weekend to be there for the Monday hearing. In our brief conversation, it became obvious that he had done nothing on the case but he promised that on Monday morning, he would meet with the prosecutor prior to the hearing. We again considered firing the attorney, but alienating a person who's well connected with prosecutors and the challenges and cost of bringing new counsel up to speed made us decide to continue with this attorney. We hoped we would see an improvement in his representation in the future.

On Monday morning, we again arrived at the cafeteria at 8:15 but this time based on the attorney's past tardiness, we were less worried when he didn't show up until almost 9 a.m. This time, he came to the table and said he was going in to speak with the prosecutor. He returned a little later, and said they'd agreed to drop the felony charges but that the DUI would stand. I asked why the expiration of the Statute of Limitations hadn't prevented this (which I'd pointed out previously on the phone), and he hesitated and said, "I'll be right back." He returned with a motion to dismiss those charges, which the prosecutor had agreed to do based on the Statute of Limitations. We'll be left with no record for Ben, but he is required to take part in a program called TASC (Treatment Assessment Screening Center). We'd again been told that we'd be done by noon, but this time we'd decided to allow plenty of time so our flights aren't until the next day. This is fortunate, as the court scheduled group meetings with a person from the TASC program at 11 a.m., and again at 4 p.m.

At these meetings, it became obvious that this might be a reasonable program for those arrested on drug charges recently. The program requires random urine drug tests for a year, as well as 48 AA meetings, and 24 hours of counseling. Since Ben has invested the last 18 months in exactly these activities and much more, we asked if any of this could be waived. Had charges been filed at the time of the arrest and this process begun, everything he's completed would have applied to these requirements. We've already spent significant amounts of money on treatment, yet we're told that nothing that Ben has done prior to today counts for anything. Ben will incur major expense to jump through hoops for the court. We wonder whether this could have been avoided if our attorney had described Ben's treatment history to the prosecuting DA. We'll never know.

Each urinalysis will cost approximately $65, which is higher than typical because of the specific testing requirements for this program. This may result in outlays in excess of $500 per month. Counseling adds additional expense. He's also assessed several thousand dollars in fees for TASC, court costs, and additional fines. There's no way that Ben's income can support these expenses, and if payments aren't made, urinalysis and counseling requirements will continue until the fees are satisfied in full, incurring still more expense. Ben's in the system and it won't let him out easily. We remind ourselves to be thankful that charges have been dropped and that he won't have a record as long as he complies with this program. He'll do all possible to cover all of these costs, but it will be impossible for him to afford it on his own and it makes no sense for him to be in this continuous loop of continuing charges and requirements if he can't make the TASC payments, so we'll end up helping to the extent necessary.

After the huge emotional toll for all of us, over $5,000 paid by Ben and an additional $10,000+ that we fronted for travel, legal fees, court costs and mandates, I sometimes wonder if we all would have been better off simply ignoring the charges since Ben was no longer in the state where the offense occurred. We recommended that he face the charges to do the responsible thing and to avoid uncertainty and potential issues in the future. Ultimately, we felt punished for being proactive in getting Ben treatment, as well as coming forward as soon as we became aware that charges had been filed.

This is an example of system logic gone wrong. On the surface it seems logical to make the offender pay, to suffer consequences for their actions. Unfortunately, politicians promoting these programs and bureaucrats applying them have no understanding of the cascade of costs involved with compliance ranging from time off work and travel, to fines, counselors, tests, etc. When penalties are set so high that they cannot be paid, nothing is gained and the defendant is put in a position where success is nearly impossible unless family help is available.

Individuals sometimes end up in jail solely because they can't comply with requirements due to lack of funds. On top of all that, despite the fines and other expenses Ben incurred, taxpayers were left to foot the bill to cover multiple court proceedings and subsidies to the TASC program even though in Ben's case they'll do nothing but collect money and receive reports to prove what he's already proven by eighteen months of sobriety and success. In the meantime, as these cases flood the system, court dockets are backed up and unable to efficiently handle cases that truly need attention in a timely manner.

If Ben's case was the only example of this lunacy it would be less tragic. Unfortunately, this type of process happens to many people who get involved with our criminal system. In hindsight, representing Ben myself, speaking directly to the D.A., or utilizing a public defender may have minimized the issues, but with our son's freedom at risk, we attempted to take the safest route, with private counsel. Therein lies the issue. With a system in which defendants live in fear of incarceration for drug offenses, there's too much risk to speak out, so defendants end up being processed and accepting whatever is done to them. Unfortunately, many defendants don't have families, resources or competent attorneys to advocate for them, and many end up in our prison system and come out with felony records, unable to build careers or a future outside of public assistance or further crime.

Probation and the Loss of Civil Liberties:

Once charged with a crime, in order to avoid the expense and risk of a trial, plea bargains are common. After a plea agreement is negotiated, the judge has discretion as to whether to accept the plea. In reality, most do accept the plea since judges want to promote plea agreements and free court calendars, and don't want to overrule agreements made by the District Attorney and the defendant. In some jurisdictions, the judge has the legal right to hold the defendant to the guilty plea entered, while NOT accepting the terms of the plea agreement. A plea could be entered, with the judge applying any penalty available under the law for the counts to which the defendant pled guilty. This could be years in jail. In these jurisdictions, defendants have given up their right to a trial and have pled guilty, yet they have no guarantee that the State will live up to their side of the agreement.

Most plea agreements, even for misdemeanors, include probation, with rules that eliminate many basic civil liberties, frequently extending for one-two years. Periods of probation are in addition to periods of time to get agreement for a plea bargain, which can take several months. Potential incarceration during the probation period is based on *subjective* decisions of a single probation officer (agent) of what constitutes a probation violation.

While it's true that decisions of an agent can be appealed, appeal can be risky. Appeals may be denied since appeal is based on the perceptions of the agent vs. that of the 'offender' (the term utilized in probation agreements in many jurisdictions). Then, the rest of probation may be served under an irritated agent – an undesirable scenario for your son or daughter on probation.

Most agents use common sense and don't want to send people to jail, but the reality is that personality conflicts, personal situations of the agent (we all have bad days) and many other factors can impact one individual's judgment. The way the law is written and applied puts offenders' freedom into the hands of one person with subjective rules. Offenses resulting in probation don't have to be severe crimes. In 35 states, this may be the result of possessing a few joints. Consider living under provisions like those below, knowing that if one person decides that you didn't comply based on their judgment, the result could be going to jail.

1. Many provisions are so subjective that it would be nearly impossible for an offender to effectively argue if an agent says the requirement wasn't complied with:

"You shall inform your agent of your whereabouts and activities as he/she directs.

You shall provide true and correct information verbally and in writing, in response to inquiries by the agent.

You shall follow any specific rules that may be issued by an agent to achieve the goals and objectives of your supervision. The rules may be modified at any time, as appropriate.

You shall submit a written report monthly and any other such relevant information as directed by your agent." (Not only subjective, but if the offender has poor organizational or writing skills, it could result in jail.)

2. The defendant's freedom and lifestyle is in the hands of the agent for the extent of the probation, with few rights of privacy.

If the defendant resides with parents, the parents' home is subject to search without notice at any time, punishing parents for providing a home for the adult child. If alcohol or firearms are in the home, it could be considered a probation violation. A gathering in the parents' home where alcohol is served could create a probation violation for the offender, even if alcohol had nothing to do with the offense, and even though the offender is not consuming alcohol. Most probation officers won't enforce these rules in regard to the parents' home, but rules of probation typically give them the legal right to do so.

Drug testing can provide positive structure, but long term, the cost, time requirements, and procedures can become problematic. Urine tests require individuals to urinate with someone observing, and if anxiety causes issues with producing urine within the time period allowed, the test is typically considered a 'fail'. Alternate forms of testing are generally not offered or accepted. Testing is required to be completed within limited time windows, with notice given each morning of that day's requirements. This can create major issues with coordinating work schedules.

For those working night shifts and then having to wake up to check requirements and comply, insomnia issues may be created. Drug testing makes sense for those new to recovery or periodically for others, but the one-size-fits-all application of the law can raise havoc with day-to-day living, can exacerbate anxiety and other issues, negatively impact self-esteem, and interfere with an individual's ability to pursue positive life goals.

Typical probation rules include:

"You shall make yourself available for searches or tests ordered by your agent including but not limited to urinalysis, breathalyzer, DNA collection and blood samples or search of residence or any property under your control.

You shall not enter into or be on the premises of any bars, taverns, liquor stores, beer tents or establishments where the primary source of income comes from the sale of alcoholic beverages.

You shall not associate with or be around any persons that are actively using or possessing alcohol or illegal drugs."

3. Should possession of a joint or a pain pill remove a person's right to change jobs, to move, to change vehicles, or to apply for credit without permission for an extended period of time? Restrictions in typical probation agreements are stringent:

"You shall not change residence or employment unless you get approval in advance from your agent, or in the case of emergency, notify your agent of the change within 72 hours.

You shall not purchase, trade, sell or operate a motor vehicle unless you get approval in advance from your agent.

You shall not borrow money or purchase on credit unless you get approval in advance from your agent."

4. Fees for probation fall on the offender, along with court costs and fines. If fees aren't paid, it can result in jail time and/or extensions of probation, creating still more costs and requirements – a true downward, perpetual spiral. Meetings and other mandates of probation can also jeopardize the offender's ability to hold a job. Too frequently, parents whose finances have already been decimated by treatment, counseling, testing and other costs are faced with also helping their children to cover these costs in order to extract them from the system and give them a chance at a fresh start.

"You shall pay monthly supervision fees as directed by your agent. You shall pay court obligations as directed by the agent."

5. While it's a noble goal for offenders to be fully employed or to go to school, requiring this as a condition of probation can be problematic. Economic conditions and the provisions of the Affordable Care Act have converted many full time positions into part time jobs. At the same time that a public record and ongoing requirements of meetings with the probation officer make full time employment more difficult to obtain, failure to comply can result in jail. Meetings are mandatory and may compromise employment either because of scheduling difficulties, or because the offender is forced to notify the employer that s/he is on probation to explain the need to take time off. This is not a way to endear oneself to an employer.

School is also a great goal, but student loans are not available if there's a felony conviction, and for other addicts, admission to school, qualifying for loans or covering costs may simply not be feasible. The 'shall' in the rule again threatens the offender with jail for something he or she may not be able to comply with.

"You shall obtain and maintain full-time employment, school or a combination of both."

Conviction records, including the terms of plea agreements, are published in the newspaper in many jurisdictions. If negotiations on the plea are delayed, this publication can occur long after the offense, creating obstacles and humiliation for individuals who've worked to proceed down a positive path since the offense occurred. Plea agreements sometimes make offenses sound more serious than they are. I've observed cases where possession of one drug resulted in multiple charges. When the choice is jail or a plea – even if the plea is severe and not representative of the offense, most offenders choose the plea. The terms of the plea being published in the local newspaper and the Internet can severely impact career opportunities.

Recovery vs. Criminal Law:

As the parents of two addicts, we were fully immersed in the recovery community. It's distressing to see that the successful techniques used in treatment are nearly the exact opposite of the techniques used in our criminal justice system.

Treatment promotes honesty. In our criminal system, speaking without representation, sharing past issues, or saying the wrong thing can have grave results. The system cultivates distrust and fear. Taxpayer funds are used to subsidize the cost of court-mandated counseling, yet offenders fear opening up to these counselors, resulting in wasted time and money in many cases.

Treatment teaches the importance of taking personal responsibility for your past, present and future actions. Our criminal system takes responsibility from individuals, whether through incarceration or through being required to get permission for daily living.

Treatment recognizes the importance of having hope and building self-esteem. The criminal justice system destroys hope and self-esteem, consistently sending the message "you aren't important", "you are flawed", "you are unworthy". The requirement of obtaining a probation officer's permission for many life activities for an extended period of time, the constant threat of jail hanging over your head, being subjected to mandatory court appearances (and accompanying attorney's fees) month after month at the whim of the prosecutor or mandatory meetings with probation officers – all leave offenders in a state of fear, shame, and low self-esteem. Living with a permanent public record requires constant explanation, apology and ongoing challenges in many aspects of life. This can be exhausting, and is the antithesis of building hope and self-esteem.

Treatment focuses on building strong, healthy relationships with family. The criminal system wears families out, destroys finances and adds incredible stress.

Treatment promotes financial responsibility and working toward achievable and fulfilling goals. The criminal system puts unreasonable financial demands on offenders, with threats of jail if fees, fines and costs aren't paid on time, and makes it nearly impossible for individuals to get ahead financially. Many simply give up.

Treatment provides a foundation of appreciation and gratitude. The criminal justice system creates fear, fatigue and resentment.

The criminal justice system impacted us in very personal ways. Our family embraced recovery – financially and emotionally, and we saw incredible success because of that commitment. The criminal justice system was too disorganized to bring charges until fifteen months after the incident, so after the focus on recovery, we saw our son lose some of the gains we'd seen him achieve. When we invested sweat, tears and retirement funds and our son invested over a year of his life to turn himself around and to convert from an active addict to a productive citizen, seeing the criminal justice system tear some of that apart became very personal. I hope that our insight might spare someone else some heartbreak or help legislators or court personnel to understand the destructive impact of what may be well-intentioned law.

Our experience was not an isolated example. This type of dysfunction is, unfortunately, a common occurrence under our present system. Our experiences and my research opened my eyes to the true cost of the 'War on Drugs'.

The War On Drugs

Drugs can destroy lives – Sometimes in large, crashing, devastating ways, and sometimes in a slow, nearly undetectable but perhaps more devastating way. Drugs have created intense, excruciating pain for our family. Because of the way drugs have touched us personally, many assume that I'd be a proponent for the War on Drugs. We've experienced it firsthand. There's nothing theoretical about the War on Drugs for me. The truth is that this so-called 'War' destroys and costs lives and has been a catastrophic failure. The statistics prove it, and our personal experience confirms it.

Many politicians believe in the theory that throwing lots of taxpayer money at an issue and locking up huge percentages of the population will somehow protect our children and solve the drug issue. The 'War on Drugs' is driven by emotion and sometimes by pure political posturing. If logic and statistics were considered, the approach would be different. Begun in 1971 when President Nixon signed the Comprehensive Drug Abuse Prevention and Control Act, the War on Drugs has been an utter failure. The initial budget for this 'war' was $100 million. Now it's $15.1 billion, with little to show except destroyed lives, large numbers of incarcerated citizens, and violent drug cartels.

Let's look at the facts:

1. Due to the Drug War, the U.S. now has the highest percentage of population in jail in the world. According to the NAACP Criminal

Justice Fact Sheet, in 2013 the U.S. comprises 5% of the world population and has 25% of the world's prisoners. A Pew Research study entitled '*One in 31, The Long Reach of American Corrections*' shows that if we combine the people in prison and jail with those under parole or on probation, **one in every 31 adults, or one in every 18 men in the U.S. is under some form of correctional control.** Studies show that jail time tends to increase drug abuse. Incarcerating hundreds of thousands of people is not minimizing drug use.

Incarceration for drug offenses has increased 12-fold from 40,000 in 1981 to nearly 500,000 by 2010, accounting for two-thirds of the rise in federal inmate population since 1985. By 2010, 51% of all inmates in federal prisons were convicted of drug-related crimes. As pointed out by former President Jimmy Carter, in some cases, criminal drug penalties can be more damaging to an individual than the use of the drug itself. This can definitely be the case when you consider the number of people who end up with felonies and lose years of their life in prison and come out with few career opportunities and a self-image that is less than conducive to success.

Gil Kerlikowske, the U.S. drug czar in 2013, speaking about the war on drugs with the Associated Press said, "In the grand scheme, it has not been successful. Forty years later, the concern about drugs and drug problems is, if anything, magnified, intensified." Despite that, Nick Gillespie of Reason Magazine writes "Obama has governed not merely as a standard-issue White House drug warrior but as a particularly hard-headed and hard-hearted one." The Obama administration has actually outpaced the Bush administration on dispensary raids, and has continued or expanded programs that funnel billions of dollars to oppressive drug-war operations in Asia and Mexico. This is quite different than Mr. Obama's posture when running for the U.S. Senate in 2004 when he said, "We need to rethink how we are operating in the drug wars and I think currently we are not doing a good job."

Our drug policy has been devastating to minorities. According to the NAACP, the United States has a higher percent of imprisoned minorities than any other country in the world. In Washington D.C., three out of every four young black men are expected to serve some time in prison. In major cities across the country, 80% of young African Americans now have criminal records.

2. Making drug trafficking illegal has made it infinitely more profitable, corrupting police and politicians and bolstering the Mexican drug cartels, which now control 90% of the drugs that enter the U.S. The drug war has had many casualties as the cartels fight over this lucrative business. In a 2007 report to Congress entitled 'Mexico's Drug Cartels', analysts estimated that wholesale earnings from illicit drug sales range from $13.6 billion to $49.4 billion annually. Ten percent of Mexico's economy is now built on drug proceeds. Big business and huge profits create corruption and promote violence.

3. The War on Drugs is an incredible drain on taxpayers with no measurable success to show for it and plenty of failure. Alcohol prohibition was a failure. Drug prohibition is no different. The U.S. has spent a trillion dollars of taxpayer money on the War on Drugs since its inception in 1971, and that's not counting the impact of lost productivity and compromised future productivity and costs related to those we lock up. A study by Cato, a libertarian think tank, showed that legalizing drugs would save the U.S. about $41 billion a year *just in drug enforcement costs*. LEAP (Law Enforcement Against Prohibition) estimates the annual cost of the drug war in the U.S. at $70 billion. LEAP is made up of current and former police, prosecutors, judges, FBI/DEA agents, corrections officials, military officers and others who, the organization says "fought on the front lines of the War on Drugs and who know firsthand that prohibition only worsens drug addiction and illicit drug market violence."

According to a study by Pew Research Center, the cost to incarcerate an inmate for a year is $30,000. Incarceration for non-violent drug offenses has been unsuccessful in reducing drug use, ruins lives, and uses resources that could be applied more beneficially elsewhere.

One of the biggest challenges is finding the funding for treatment for addicts. Surely spending $30,000/year for incarceration isn't the best allocation of funds in these cases.

What do we have to show for this cost and other negative cascade effects of pursuing this 'War'? A May 13, 2010 Associated Press article based on Freedom of Information Act requests, archival records, federal budgets and dozens of interviews with leaders and analysts, the AP concluded "After 40 years, $1 trillion, U.S. War on Drugs has failed to meet any of its goals." Still, we continue to pour money into this failure with dismal results.

According to the World Health Organization, the U.S. is the number one nation in the world in illegal drug use. LEAP says "Despite all the lives destroyed and all the money so ill spent, today illicit drugs are cheaper, more potent, and much easier to access than they were at the beginning of the War on Drugs." According to the Bureau of Justice Statistics, two thirds of prisoners will reoffend. Limitations on gainful employment and other opportunities after doing jail time are partly to blame for this high recidivism rate. Infectious diseases are also highly concentrated in prisons. All in all, it's not a place that any of us want our children to experience. The War on Drugs is sacrificing more and more of our youth based on these policies.

4. The War on Drugs shows enormous hypocrisy and teaches our children disdain for the law. Is it any mystery why our children have less respect for the law than our generation, when they see the hypocrisy of their friends being locked up for doing what the three most recent Presidents of the United States have done? Barack Obama in his book *Dreams from My Father* stated that he "drank heavily," "tried drugs enthusiastically," and tried "a little blow when you could afford it." In a 2008 interview, then Senator Obama, in response to a question about drug use, laughed and stated 'I inhaled frequently . . . that was the whole point'. George W. Bush was arrested for DUI at age 30 when his license was suspended for two years. He also allegedly stated in a taped conversation with a friend "I wouldn't answer the

marijuana question. You know why? I don't want some little kid doing what I tried." Bill Clinton's admission to smoking marijuana was famously followed by his 'I didn't inhale' statement. There have been allegations that Presidents Obama, Bush, and Clinton all experimented with cocaine. Perhaps the good news is that, even if our children have drug histories, they may still become President. The bad news is that the escalation of the War on Drugs by all of these presidents increases the chances that a child may end up a felon or an ex-con. To date, that has put a damper on career opportunities.

More hypocrisy exists in the medical marijuana farce. Anyone who's walked down Venice Beach, California knows that getting a medical marijuana card is available to the general public. Is there really benefit in making people jump through hoops for the same outcome as outright legalization? What logic or morality can explain the pick and choose nature of federal raids on medical marijuana dispensaries where one shop can operate untouched while another owner spends long periods of time in jail? Doesn't all of this simply increase disdain for our laws and drain law enforcement and prison budgets that should be spent to deal with violent crime?

Part of the challenge with criminal justice system reform is that individuals who experience it have little credibiity in the eyes of those in a position to create change. Additionally, those 'experiencing' the system are afraid to speak up in fear of negative consequences from prosecutors with whom they're negotiating, probation or parole officers who have the power to incarcerate them, or prison officials who can severely impact their lives. It's easy for those not personally impacted to think "It can't be that bad. These people broke the law and should accept their punishment." Experiencing the system changes that perspective.

From a personal standpoint, excessive family resources were wasted in legal theatrics to keep our sons out of jail. Throughout this process I was very aware that, had our sons not been fortunate to have parents who could help them navigate the system, their lives would have been much different, and they would almost certainly have spent time behind bars with felony records. The criminal justice system caused enormous emotional strain and financial drain for us. Our sons staying out of jail has not jeopardized the public, and has allowed them to become productive members of society. Unfortunately, the resources spent on maneuvering through the legal quagmire were not available to help them or ourselves for more productive uses – whether to protect our retirement, to pay for their treatment, or to help them to start businesses or other opportunities that may have created jobs or otherwise benefited the community.

During our sons' active use, I also lost sleep worrying about illegal drug buys that could go wrong or drugs laced with other ingredients. Legalization would minimize these risks.

Our children began drug use in high school. At that time, it was easier for them to get pot than to get alcohol. The illegal nature of the pot immediately put them into contact with dealers who not only sold pot, but also offered other drugs. Since the law was already being broken, it was less of a step for the kids to escalate their drug use. I'm not defending our sons' illegal activity, but it is time for us, as a country, to realize that our current laws have failed to achieve the goals for which they were passed. Instead, we are spending huge amounts of taxpayer money, locking up hundreds of thousands of people, and ruining lives.

So what can be done? Assessing what's worked elsewhere would be a good start. In 2001, Portugal legalized all drugs within its borders largely to control their HIV epidemic. At the time, many predicted disaster, but more than a decade later, drug use in Portugal has dramatically declined. A Cato study found that "freeing its citizens from the fear of prosecution and imprisonment for drug usage, Portugal has dramatically improved its ability to encourage drug addicts to avail themselves of treatment. The resources that were previously devoted to prosecuting and imprisoning drug addicts are now available to provide treatment programs to addicts." According to that study "the majority of European Union states have rates that are double and triple the rate for post-decriminalization Portugal".

For me, after watching our sons suffer from addiction, the statistics are profound. After decriminalization, Portugal's marijuana usage in people over 15 dropped to about 10% (compared to 40% of people over 12 in the U.S. where we have some of the strictest drug laws in the world). Drug use of all types declined in Portugal. Lifetime use among seventh-to-ninth grade students declined from 14.01% to 10.6%, and lifetime heroin use in the 16-18 year old age group fell from 2.5% to 1.8%. I like that trend. Had we been part of those statistics, perhaps our family could have been spared. If the U.S. could come close to duplicating those statistics, think of how many families would escape the misery caused by the high incidents of drug addiction in the U.S. under our current law. Our current system simply isn't working.

When I was 20 years old, the drinking age in our state was lowered from 21 to 18. With the change in law, it was much less exciting to go to the bars than when it was against the law. At that age, prohibition adds glamour and attracts youth. Perhaps saving taxpayer funds, reducing prison populations and refocusing efforts to a treatment-based, rather than prosecution-based model would also take some of the glamour out of our teens' initial experimentation with drugs. It time to allocate parental and government resources to treatment rather than to punishment for victimless crimes. It's time to end the fiasco called the 'War on Drugs'.

PART 3 –
LIFE CONTINUES
OR
"RELAPSE & REFLECTIONS"

"The mightiest oak in the forest is just a little nut that held its ground."
-Another favorite fortune cookie

CHAPTER 25

RELAPSE

BEN HAS RETURNED home and is living with us for now. The Port Townsend experience was a wonderful one, but the cost of living made it difficult to get ahead and as friends moved on, Ben decided it would be nice to return home to be closer to friends and family. It's been therapeutic having him home, has allowed us to get reacquainted on an adult level and is helping him to build a financial foundation. It hasn't all been roses, and addiction isn't a project with a definitive end date. About a year after returning to our hometown, he relapsed. It was heart wrenching, but the world didn't fall apart, and after a wakeup call for him including a lost job and more drug possession charges, he made use of what he'd learned in recovery and put his life back together.

My initial panic when we became aware of the relapse was "We simply can't afford the cost of another treatment in terms of money or emotional energy." Our discussion with Ben following the relapse was less hysterical on my part than would have been the case in earlier days. Ben's comments also gave me confidence. "Mom, I know what I need to do. It's my responsibility." We're going with that, and we're hopeful.

With drug use on and off since adolescence, it has been difficult to accurately diagnose and treat Ben's ADD and other symptoms. A few months after his relapse, he approached us about getting help.

With his renewed commitment to sobriety, he was able to successfully work with our family physician and is currently on ADD medication, which has made a huge difference in his ability to focus and has calmed the hyperactivity. We believe this will help him in maintaining his sobriety, in addition to living a happier, fuller life.

It's always a challenge to know whether drugs should be used to treat secondary issues when addiction is a factor. In our experience, it's worth the risk. For the initial appointment to discuss medications, we accompanied Ben to the physician. We laid out the history for the doctor and expressed our support for prescribing medications at this time. Showing family support and letting the physician know that we'd be involved in monitoring results made him more comfortable in prescribing. For us, seeing the impact of the medication on Ben helps us to understand why he was trying to self-medicate. With the medication, he's more relaxed, less fidgety and more able to focus. We are cautiously optimistic that he's finally found the right medication. Having it prescribed legally solves a multitude of issues.

Ben has started a specialty food business and is excited about his future. Our advice has been, "Figure out what the steps are, and work your plan." Sounds like a strategy he's familiar with. Continuing to work on his sobriety, rebuilding his finances, and proving to himself and others that he can handle responsibility while maintaining the balance needed for sobriety are all steps in the right direction. He's on track. In all honesty, the relapse made me hyperventilate a bit and set me back, bringing back emotions and fears I hadn't felt for a long time. I worried more after the relapse, but as time passed, the worry has subsided. It was reassuring to see that the world didn't fall apart when it happened and that he came back from it and returned to sobriety. It also gave me hope that another relapse won't happen, or if it does, that he'll handle it. Either way, it's time for us to let go.

Ben's biggest challenge at this point is dealing with the criminal consequences of the relapse. It took over ten months to negotiate a plea agreement that didn't require jail, partly because the prosecutor was pursuing a judgeship, so pushed cases back, and didn't want to look 'soft on crime'. Ultimately, Ben ended up on probation for two years. The terms of probation require full time work, but the counselor mandated by the probation officer has been adamant that he should focus full time on recovery and should not work. Inconsistent mandates and recommendations abound within the system.

At the point of these discussions, Ben had been clean and sober for four years except for the relapse thirteen months prior. The counselor didn't expound on how long she recommended not working, or how he was to support himself or to pay the fees assessed for her – and other – probation services. I have great respect for focusing on recovery, but life also needs to be lived. As a taxpayer, I fear that these attitudes unnecessarily push people into public assistance, and dissuade them from pursuing positive goals. Ben chose not to follow that recommendation.

Ben is also required to attend a multi-day class on integration into the community, which includes a tour of the Farmers' Market. In order to attend this required class, he will have to take the day off from working his own booth – *at that same Farmers' Market*. It would be impossible to make up anything as absurd as the application of this system.

Long-term lifestyle choices will be different for our sons. After three years of sobriety, Michael let us know that he planned to have a few drinks on New Year's and that he wanted to test social drinking. After the hell we'd been through and had watched him endure, it was difficult not to panic. Statistics don't encourage optimism. Drinking after battling a drug addiction is dangerous, and for the vast majority of people can have horrendous consequences.

Bottom line for us was that the decision was his to make – not ours. We knew that his life was working and that the people with whom he associates, where he lives and his entire lifestyle had completely changed since the days of his drug use. After our hearts started beating again, with some trepidation we thanked him for giving us a heads up and we gave him our blessing to do what he believed would work for him. Six years later, this still seems to be working for him. Michael's social drinking should NOT provide anyone reading this with rationalization to follow in his footsteps. With all the pain associated with addiction, there's no doubt that it's safest to stay completely clean.

My guess is that Ben will need to stay drug and alcohol free (except for prescribed medications) for long-term sobriety, and he's chosen to do that since his relapse. He's never been much of a drinker, but painkillers will likely be an ongoing issue for him and if he uses pot, alcohol, or anything else that lets his guard down, the risk of relapse on painkillers will increase. Only he can find ways to take care of himself and find balance.

Our sons know what they need to do. They have to make their own individual choices for long-term success. We believe they will.

CONCLUSION

FOR ME, THE most difficult change was the permanent loss of inno-
cence. It's inevitable for everyone, I suppose, but until the addictions
I'd lived my life believing that there were some things that would
simply never touch my life. There was a line in the sand, and I never
thought or worried about the things on the 'other side' of that line.
Seeing my children addicted to drugs was on the other side of that
line. It frustrates me that, in my honeymoon of life where the soft
blanket of naiveté protected me, I had little appreciation for it. I didn't
realize at the time that life's future lessons would open the floodgates
– forcing me to realize that life can bring unimaginable sorrow and
that living it and surviving through it are the only option. As with
many of life's lessons, despite causing pain, stepping over that line in
the sand expanded my perceptions and opened my heart.

Until that time, I hadn't felt the full joy that comes with a warm
breeze, a Black-Eyed Susan in bloom, or a cold glass of ice water in
a crystal glass while, for that moment, I'm at peace – whether all's
well with the world or not. Until that time, I also hadn't been able to
fully understand or empathize with people who'd experienced life's
traumas. The 'addiction' experience made me less judgmental, *living*
the principal of 'never judge til you walk in another's shoes', rather
than just thinking that's a nice theory. It's opened empathy that living
through trauma brings. I have a new appreciation for the strength
and the heart it takes to thrive, and some days, just to survive. I've
survived the unthinkable, and if you have an addicted child, you're

still standing and you're reading this, then YOU have survived! I now know that I'm better equipped for the future, but also, on most days, have better learned to relish the present. If someone treats me badly, I can now understand that it likely has little to do with me, and a lot to do with his or her own survival mechanisms. When in crisis, I was not always gracious, logical, or courteous and it had NOTHING to do with the recipient of my mood. I can now appreciate that I have no idea what others may be experiencing. My greatest gift to myself and to others is to be understanding, supportive and non-judgmental, and to live my own life to its fullest.

Do I worry? Yes, the line has been crossed and the list of disasters that I now acknowledge could happen has been permanently expanded. My confidence in my capacity to deal with whatever comes has also increased.

I still worry about our sons and relapse is a consideration, but understanding the level of wisdom gained through their hard work balances that. Most days I'm now a typical Mom of adult children, loving them, being amazed by them, and worrying about them. They crossed their lines in the sand early in life, experiencing the demons and the trauma inherent with addiction in ways far different from my experience as their Mom. They saw the harsher side of life at early ages. They've seen friends die, others relapse, and others spend years in jail, and I'm sure they've experienced many other things I'll never know about and perhaps wouldn't want to know. But at an early age, they also have a better understanding than I did about the fragility of life and the importance of treasuring the moments, living and loving fully, taking the time to smell the flowers and feel the breeze, and pouring their heart and soul into their passions.

Above all, I treasure my relationships with Steve, Ben, Michael, and now Sarah, Michael's wife. They're independent and have their own lives, but perhaps like surviving hell week in a fraternity initiation, we're closer because of all we went through. Having your guts ripped out together makes minor scrapes more trivial and easier to deal with, and minimizes the need for secrets or pretense. As we move toward the inevitable role reversal that happens with generations, I already seek wisdom and advice from them at times, and find it easier to reel in my instinct and tendency to over-advise and over-protect. My fluffy blanket of naiveté has been traded in for a huge, tattered and holey, soft, warm, and cozy blanket of love.

APPENDICES

APPENDIX A - Groups And Organizations Supporting Recovery

APPENDIX B – What's It Like To Have ADD?

APPENDIX C – Co-Dependents Anonymous, Inc. Chart 'Recovery Patterns of Codependence'

ONLINE RESOURCES

See www.AddictsMomBook.com for the following resources:

Treatment Centers, Aftercare Programs & University Programs
Groups and Organizations Supporting Recovery
Sample Contracts For Teen or Adult Child Living At Home
Sample Letters To Addicted Child
Durable Financial Power of Attorney
HIPAA
Authorization For Release Of Information

GROUPS AND ORGANIZATIONS SUPPORTING RECOVERY

Associations and Other Groups:

Alcoholics Anonymous; Phone: 212-870-3400
Address: P.O. Box 459, Grand Central Station, New York, NY 10163
Website: www.aa.org; (Provides links to locate meetings
worldwide.)

Narcotics Anonymous; Phone: 818-773-9999
Address: P.O. Box 9999, Van Nuys, California 91409
Email: customer_service@na.org
Website: www.na.org

Families Anonymous (for families and friends of those with drug, alcohol
or related behavioral issues)
Phone: 800-736-9805 (US only), or 847-294-5877
Address: 701 Lee St., Suite 670, Des Plaines, IL 60016
Website: www.familiesanonymous.org

Al-Anon and Alateen ; Phone: 757-563-1600
Address: 1600 Corporate Landing Parkway Virginia Beach, VA
23454-5617
Email: afgwso@al-anon.org
Website: http://al-anon.alateen.org

Codependents Anonymous (CoDa); Phone: 888-444-2359 or
602-277-7991
Address: P.O. Box 33577, Phoenix, Arizona 85067-3577
Email: outreach@coda.org
Website: www.coda.org

Adult ADD Association; Phone: (206)-647-6681
Address: 1225 E. Sunset Dr. #640, Bellingham, WA 98226-3529
Email: poast@prodigy.net
Website: http://www.healthsupportcenter.org/aadda/

CHADD (Children and Adults with Attention-Deficit/Hyperactivity
Disorder)
Phone: 800-233-4050 or 301-306-7070
Address: 8181 Professional Place – Suite 150, Landover, MN 20785
Website: www.chadd.org

WHAT'S IT LIKE TO HAVE ADD?

THE FOLLOWING ARTICLE by Edward M. Hallowell, M.D (author of Driven to Distraction, ©1994), is the best I've read to describe attention deficit and its effect on the individual and the family. It's included here because ADD frequently coexists with addiction. Ben laughed all the way through this article, saying he recognized himself in nearly every line. This also describes Steve.

What's It Like to Have ADD?

What is it like to have ADD? What is the feel of the syndrome? I have a short talk that I often give to groups as an introduction to the subjective experience of ADD and what it is like to live with it:

Attention Deficit Disorder. First of all I resent the term. As far as I'm concerned most people have Attention Surplus Disorder. I mean, life being what it is, who can pay attention to anything for very long? Is it really a sign of mental health to be able to balance your checkbook, sit still in your chair, and never speak out of turn? As far as I can see, many people who don't have ADD are charter members of the Congenitally Boring.

But anyway, be that as it may, there is this syndrome called ADD or ADHD, depending on what book you read. So what's it like to have

ADD? Some people say the so-called syndrome doesn't even exist, but believe me, it does. Many metaphors come to mind to describe it. It's like driving in the rain with bad windshield wipers. Everything is smudged and blurred and you're speeding along, and it's reeeealyy frustrating not being able to see very well. Or it's like listening to a radio station with a lot of static and you have to strain to hear what's going on. Or, it's like trying to build a house of cards in a dust storm. You have to build a structure to protect yourself from the wind before you can even start on the cards.

In other ways it's like being super-charged all the time. You get one idea and you have to act on it, and then, what do you know, but you've got another idea before you've finished up with the first one, and so you go for that one, but of course a third idea intercepts the second, and you just have to follow that one, and pretty soon people are calling you disorganized and impulsive and all sorts of impolite words that miss the point completely. Because you're trying really hard. It's just that you have all these invisible vectors pulling you this way and that which makes it really hard to stay on task.

Plus which, you're spilling over all the time. You're drumming your fingers, tapping your feet, humming a song, whistling, looking here, looking there, scratching, stretching, doodling, and people think you're not paying attention or that you're not interested, but all you're doing is spilling over so that you can pay attention. I can pay a lot better attention when I'm taking a walk or listening to music or even when I'm in a crowded, noisy room than when I'm still and surrounded by silence. God save me from the reading rooms. Have you ever been into the one in Widener Library? The only thing that saves it is that so many of the people who use it have ADD that there's a constant, soothing bustle.

What is it like to have ADD? Buzzing. Being here and there and everywhere. Someone once said, "Time is the thing that keeps everything from happening all at once." Time parcels moments out into separate bits so that we can do one thing at a time. In ADD, this does not happen. In ADD, time collapses. Time becomes a black hole. To the person with ADD it feels as if everything is happening all at once. This creates a sense of inner turmoil or even panic. The individual loses perspective and the ability to prioritize. He or she is always on the go, trying to keep the world from caving in on top.

Museums. (Have you noticed how I skip around? That's part of the deal. I change channels a lot. And radio stations. Drives my wife nuts. "Can't we listen to just one song all the way through?") Anyway, museums. The way I go through a museum is the way some people go through Filene's basement. Some of this, some of that, oh, this one looks nice, but what about that rack over there? Gotta hurry, gotta run. It's not that I don't like art. I love art. But my way of loving it makes most people think I'm a Philistine. On the other hand, sometimes I can sit and look at one painting for a long while. I'll get into the world of the painting and buzz around in there until I forget about everything else. In these moments I, like most people with ADD, can hyperfocus, which gives the lie to the notion that we can never pay attention. Sometimes we have turbocharged focusing abilities. It just depends upon the situation.

Lines. I'm almost incapable of waiting in lines. I just can't wait, you see. That's the hell of it. Impulse leads to action. I'm very short on what you might call the intermediate reflective step between impulse and action. That's why I, like so many people with ADD, lack tact. Tact is entirely dependent on the ability to consider one's words before uttering them. We ADD types don't do this so well. I remember in the fifth grade I noticed my math teacher's hair in a new style and blurted out, "Mr. Cook, it that a toupe you're wearing?" I got kicked out of class. I've since learned how to say these inappropriate things in such a way or at such a time that they can in fact be helpful. But it has taken time. That's the thing about ADD. It takes a lot of adapting to get on in life. But it certainly can be done, and be done very well.

As you might imagine, intimacy can be a problem if you've got to be constantly changing the subject, pacing, scratching and blurting out tactless remarks. My wife has learned not to take my tuning out personally, and she says that when I'm there, I'm really there. At first, when we met, she thought I was some kind of a nut, as I would bolt out of restaurants at the end of meals or disappear to another planet during a conversation. Now she has grown accustomed to my sudden coming and goings.

Many of us with ADD crave high-stimulus situations. In my case, I love the racetrack. And I love the high-intensity crucible of doing psychotherapy. And I love having lots of people around. Obviously this tendency can get you into trouble, which is why ADD is high among criminals and self-destructive risk-takers. It is also high among so-called Type A personalities, as well as among manic-depressives, sociopaths and criminals, violent people, drug abusers, and alcoholics. But it is also high among creative and intuitive people in all fields, and among highly energetic, highly productive people.

Which is to say there is a positive side to all this. Usually the positive doesn't get mentioned when people speak about ADD because there is a natural tendency to focus on what goes wrong, or at least on what has to be somehow controlled. But often once the ADD has been diagnosed, and the child or the adult, with the help of teachers and parents or spouses, friends, and colleagues, has learned how to cope with it, an untapped realm of the brain swims into view. Suddenly the radio station is tuned in, the windshield is clear, the sand storm has died down. And the child or adult, who had been such a problem, such a nudge, such a general pain in the neck to himself and everybody else, that person starts doing things he'd never been able to do before. He surprises everyone around him, and he surprises himself.

I use the male pronoun, but it could just as easily be she, as we are seeing more and more ADD among females as we are looking for it.

Often these people are highly imaginative and intuitive. They have a "feel" for things, a way of seeing right into the heart of matters while others have to reason their way along methodically. This is the person who can't explain how he thought of the solution, or where the idea for the story came from, or why suddenly he produced such a painting, or how he knew the short cut to the answer, but all he can say is he just knew it, he could feel it. This is the man or woman who makes million dollar deals in a catnap and pulls them off the next day. This is the child who, having been reprimanded for blurting something out, is then praised for having blurted out something brilliant. These are the people who learn and know and do and go by touch and feel.

These people can feel a lot. In places where most of us are blind, they can, if not see the light, at least feel the light, and they can produce answers apparently out of the dark. It is important for others to be sensitive to this "sixth sense" many ADD people have, and to nurture it. If the environment insists on rational, linear thinking and "good" behavior from these people all the time, then they may never develop their intuitive style to the point where they can use it profitably. It can be exasperating to listen to people talk. They can sound so vague or rambling. But if you take them seriously and grope along with them, often you will find they are on the brink of startling conclusions or surprising solutions.

What I am saying is that their cognitive style is qualitatively different from most people's, and what may seem impaired, with patience and encouragement may become gifted.

The thing to remember is that if the diagnosis can be made, then most of the bad stuff associated with ADD can be avoided or contained. The diagnosis can be liberating, particularly for people who have been stuck with labels like, "lazy", "stubborn", "willful", "disruptive", "impossible", "tyrannical", "a spaceshot", "brain damaged", "stupid", or just plain "bad". Making the diagnosis of ADD can take the case from the court of moral judgment to the clinic of neuropsychiatric treatment.

What is the treatment all about? Anything that turns down the noise. Just making the diagnosis helps turn down the noise of guilt and self-recrimination. Building certain kinds of structure into one's life can help a lot. Working in small spurts rather than long hauls. Breaking tasks down into smaller tasks. Making lists. Getting help where you need it, whether it's having a secretary, or an accountant, or an automatic bank teller, or a good filing system, or a home computer - getting help where you need it. Maybe applying external limits on your impulses. Or getting enough exercise to work off some of the noise inside. Finding support. Getting someone in your corner to coach you, to keep you on track. Medication can help a great deal too, but it is far from the whole solution. The good news is that treatment can really help.

Let me leave you by telling you that we need your help and understanding. We may make mess-piles wherever we go, but with your help, those mess-piles can be turned into realms of reason and art. So, if you know someone like me who's acting up and daydreaming and forgetting this or that and just not getting with the program consider ADD before he starts believing all the bad things people are saying about him and it's too late.

The main point of the talk is that there is a more complex subjective experience to ADD than a list of symptoms can possibly impart. ADD is a way of life, and until recently it has been hidden, even from the view of those who have it. The human experience of ADD is more than just a collection of symptoms. It is a way of living. Before the syndrome is diagnosed, that way of living may be filled with pain and misunderstanding. After the diagnosis is made, one often finds new possibilities and the chance for real change.

The adult syndrome of ADD, so long unrecognized, is now at last bursting upon the scene. Thankfully, millions of adults who have had to think of themselves as defective or unable to get their acts together, will instead be able to make the most of their considerable abilities. It is a hopeful time indeed.

Reprinted with permission of Edward M. Hallowell, M.D., author of Driven to Distraction, © 1994, Superparenting for ADD, © 2008, Worry, ©1998 and several other books.

RECOVERY PATTERNS OF CODEPENDENCE

	Codependents often...	In Recovery...
Denial Patterns	Have difficulty identifying what they are feeling	I am aware of my feelings and identify them, often in the moment. I know the difference between my thoughts and feelings.
	Minimize, alter, or deny how they truly feel.	I embrace my feelings; they are valid and important.
	Perceive themselves as completely unselfish and dedicated to the well-being of others	I know the difference between caring and caretaking. I recognize that caretaking others is often motivated by a need to benefit myself.
	Lack empathy for the feelings and needs of others.	I am able to feel compassion for another's feelings and needs.
	Label others with their negative traits.	I acknowledge that I may own the negative traits I often perceive in others.
	Think they can take care of themselves without any help from others.	I acknowledge that I sometimes need the help of others.
	Mask pain in various ways such as anger, humor, or isolation.	I am aware of my painful feelings and express them appropriately.
	Express negativity or aggression in indirect and passive ways.	I am able to express my feelings openly, directly, and calmly.
	Do not recognize the unavailability of those people to whom they are attracted.	I pursue intimate relationships only with others who want, and are able to engage in, healthy and loving relationships.

	Codependents often...	In Recovery...
Low Self-esteem Patterns	Have difficulty making decisions.	I trust my ability to make effective decisions.
	Judge what they think, say, or do harshly, as never good enough.	I accept myself as I am. I emphasize progress over perfection.
	Are embarrassed to receive recognition, praise, or gifts.	I feel appropriately worthy of the recognition, praise, or gifts I receive.
	Value others' approval of their thinking, feelings, and behavior over their own.	I value the opinions of those I trust, without needing to gain their approval. I have confidence in myself.
	Do not perceive themselves as lovable or worthwhile persons.	I recognize myself as being a lovable and valuable person.
	Seek recognition and praise to overcome feeling less than.	I seek my own approval first, and examine my motivations carefully when I seek approval from others.
	Have difficulty admitting a mistake.	I continue to take my personal inventory, and when I am wrong, promptly admit it.
	Need to appear to be right in the eyes of others and may even lie to look good.	I am honest with myself about my behaviors and motivations. I feel secure enough to admit mistakes to myself and others, and to hear their opinions without feeling threatened.
	Are unable to identify or ask for what they need and want.	I meet my own needs and wants when possible. I reach out for help when it's necessary and appropriate.

	Codependents often...	In Recovery...
Low Self-esteem Patterns	Perceive themselves as superior to others.	I perceive myself as equal to others.
	Look to others to provide their sense of safety.	With the help of my Higher Power, I create safety in my life.
	Have difficulty getting started, meeting deadlines, and completing projects.	I avoid procrastination by meeting my responsibilities in a timely manner.
	Have trouble setting healthy priorities and boundaries.	I am able to establish and uphold healthy priorities and boundaries in my life.
Compliance Patterns	Are extremely loyal, remaining in harmful situations too long.	I am committed to my safety and leave situations that feel unsafe or are inconsistent with my goals.
	Compromise their own values and integrity to avoid rejection or anger.	I am rooted in my own values, even if others don't agree or become angry.
	Put aside their own interests in order to do what others want.	I consider my interests and feelings when asked to participate in another's plans.
	Are hyper vigilant regarding the feelings of others and take on those feelings.	I can separate my feelings from the feelings of others. I allow myself to experience my feelings and others to be responsible for their feelings.
	Are afraid to express their beliefs, opinions, and feelings when they differ from those of others.	I respect my own opinions and feelings and express them appropriately.
	Accept sexual attention when they want love.	My sexuality is grounded in genuine intimacy and connection. When I need to feel loved, I express my heart's desires. I do not settle for sex without love.

	Codependents often...	In Recovery...
Compliance Patterns	Make decisions without regard to the consequences.	I ask my Higher Power for guidance, and consider possible consequences before I make decisions.
	Give up their truth to gain the approval of others or to avoid change.	I stand in my truth and maintain my integrity, whether others approve or not, even if it means making difficult changes in my life.
	Believe people are incapable of taking care of themselves.	I realize that, with rare exceptions, other adults are capable of managing their own lives.
Control Patterns	Attempt to convince others what to think, do, or feel.	I accept the thoughts, choices, and feelings of others, even though I may not be comfortable with them.
	Freely offer advice and direction without being asked.	I give advice only when asked
	Become resentful when others decline their help or reject their advice.	I am content to see others take care of themselves.
	Lavish gifts and favors on those they want to influence.	I carefully and honestly contemplate my motivations when preparing to give a gift.
	Use sexual attention to gain approval and acceptance.	I embrace and celebrate my sexuality as evidence of my health and wholeness. I do not use it to gain the approval of others.
	Have to feel needed in order to have a relationship with others.	I develop relationships with others based on equality, intimacy, and balance.
	Demand that their needs be met by others.	I find and use resources that meet my needs without making demands on others. I ask for help when I need it, without expectation.

	Codependents often...	In Recovery...
Control Patterns	Use charm and charisma to convince others of their capacity to be caring and compassionate.	I behave authentically with others, allowing my caring and compassionate qualities to emerge.
	Use blame and shame to exploit others emotionally.	I ask directly for what I want and need and trust the outcome to my Higher Power. I do not try to manipulate outcomes with blame or shame.
	Refuse to cooperate, compromise, or negotiate.	I cooperate, compromise, and negotiate with others in a way that honors my integrity.
	Adopt an attitude of indifference, helplessness, authority, or rage to manipulate outcomes.	I treat others with respect and consideration, and trust my Higher Power to meet my needs and desires.
	Use recovery jargon in an attempt to control the behavior of others.	I use my recovery for my own growth and not to manipulate or control others.
	Pretend to agree with others to get what they want.	My communication with others is authentic and truthful.
Avoidance Patterns	Act in ways that invite others to reject, shame, or express anger toward them.	I act in ways that encourage loving and healthy responses from others.
	Judge harshly what others think, say, or do.	I keep an open mind and accept others as they are.
	Avoid emotional, physical, or sexual intimacy as a way to maintain distance.	I engage in emotional, physical, or sexual intimacy when it is healthy and appropriate for me.
	Allow addictions to people, places, and things to distract them from achieving intimacy in relationships.	I practice my recovery to develop healthy and fulfilling relationships.

	Codependents often...	In Recovery...
Avoidance Patterns	Use indirect or evasive communication to avoid conflict or confrontation.	I use direct and straight-forward communication to resolve conflicts and deal appropriately with confrontations.
	Diminish their capacity to have healthy relationships by declining to use the tools of recovery.	When I use the tools of recovery, I am able to develop and maintain healthy relationships of my choosing.
	Suppress their feelings or needs to avoid feeling vulnerable.	I embrace my own vulnerability by trusting and honoring my feelings and needs.
	Pull people toward them, but when others get close, push them away.	I welcome close relationships while maintaining healthy boundaries.
	Refuse to give up their self-will to avoid surrendering to a power greater than themselves.	I believe in and trust a power greater than myself. I willingly surrender my self-will to my Higher Power.
	Believe displays of emotion are a sign of weakness.	I honor my authentic emotions and share them when appropriate.
	Withhold expressions of appreciation.	I freely engage in expressions of appreciation toward others.

Reprinted with permission of Co-Dependents Anonymous, Inc.

CPSIA information can be obtained at www.ICGtesting.com
Printed in the USA
LVOW13s1813160714

394635LV00020B/1328/P